Contents

How Many Frogs?

There are _____ red frogs.

There are _____ green frogs.

How many red and green frogs in all? _____

Do you add or subtract? _____

Show your work.

There is _____ big red frog.

There are _____ small red frogs.

How many more small red frogs? _____

Do you add or subtract? _____

Show your work.

How many yellow frogs? _____

How many red frogs? _____

How many green frogs? _____

How many frogs in all? _____

Do you add or subtract? _____

Show your work.

Frogs

Hopping Home

Help find Frog. Add. Color the lily pads of 8 or more green.

Start here.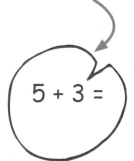

5 + 3 =

4 + 3 =

6 + 1 =

3 + 0 =

2 + 7 =

1 + 4 =

0 + 0 =

3 + 2 =

7 + 1 =

3 + 5 =

6 + 0 =

3 + 3 =

4 + 2 =

7 + 3 =

3 + 3 =

3 + 4 =

4 + 5 =

2 + 6 =

8 + 1 =

9 + 1 =

Frogs

Choose the number sentence that fits each story.

4 frogs were swimming in the pond. 3 more frogs jumped in. How many frogs in the pond in all?

4 - 3 = 1

4 + 3 = 7

7 - 4 = 3

A big yellow frog ate 6 flies. A small red frog ate 5 flies. How many more flies did the yellow frog eat?

5 - 0 = 5

6 + 5 = 11

6 - 5 = 1

Draw a picture to show each answer.

6 frogs were sitting on a log. 3 frogs hopped off. How many frogs were left on the log?

5 frogs were croaking a happy tune. 2 more frogs joined in. How many frogs were singing in all?

Frogs

Tasty Flies

How many flies did Frog eat?

8 + 1 = _____   5 + 1 = _____

3 + 5 = _____   6 + 2 = _____   6 + 4 = _____

0 + 7 = _____   0 + 8 = _____   8 + 2 = _____

6 + 3 = _____   4 + 3 = _____   1 + 5 = _____

5 + 5 = _____   7 + 3 = _____   2 + 2 = _____

1 + 3 = _____   5 + 4 = _____   2 + 5 = _____

4 + 2 = _____   3 + 3 = _____   3 + 6 = _____

*Super Bonus: How many flies did Frog eat in all? _____

Frogs

Graphs show facts and give information. This is a pictograph. It uses pictures to give information. Each picture stands for 1 animal.

Animals Who Live in the Pond

Frogs

Turtles

Snakes

Fish

How many frogs live in the pond? _____

How many turtles live in the pond? _____

How many snakes live in the pond? _____

Are there more frogs or more turtles? _____

How many more? _____

Are there more turtles or more snakes? _____

How many more? _____

Are there more fish or more frogs? _____

How many more? _____

Frogs

How Many Are Left?

$$\begin{array}{r} 4 \text{ frogs} \\ - 2 \text{ frogs} \\ \hline 2 \text{ frogs} \end{array} \qquad \begin{array}{r} 4 \\ - 2 \\ \hline 2 \end{array}$$

Subtract.

$$\begin{array}{r} 5 \\ - 3 \\ \hline \end{array} \qquad \begin{array}{r} 10 \\ - 9 \\ \hline \end{array} \qquad \begin{array}{r} 3 \\ - 3 \\ \hline \end{array} \qquad \begin{array}{r} 9 \\ - 4 \\ \hline \end{array} \qquad \begin{array}{r} 8 \\ - 2 \\ \hline \end{array}$$

$$\begin{array}{r} 8 \\ - 4 \\ \hline \end{array} \qquad \begin{array}{r} 10 \\ - 7 \\ \hline \end{array} \qquad \begin{array}{r} 6 \\ - 5 \\ \hline \end{array} \qquad \begin{array}{r} 5 \\ - 1 \\ \hline \end{array} \qquad \begin{array}{r} 6 \\ - 6 \\ \hline \end{array}$$

$$\begin{array}{r} 9 \\ - 3 \\ \hline \end{array} \qquad \begin{array}{r} 8 \\ - 5 \\ \hline \end{array} \qquad \begin{array}{r} 9 \\ - 6 \\ \hline \end{array} \qquad \begin{array}{r} 10 \\ - 5 \\ \hline \end{array} \qquad \begin{array}{r} 7 \\ - 5 \\ \hline \end{array}$$

$$\begin{array}{r} 2 \\ - 0 \\ \hline \end{array} \qquad \begin{array}{r} 4 \\ - 3 \\ \hline \end{array} \qquad \begin{array}{r} 5 \\ - 4 \\ \hline \end{array} \qquad \begin{array}{r} 6 \\ - 3 \\ \hline \end{array} \qquad \begin{array}{r} 7 \\ - 2 \\ \hline \end{array}$$

Frogs

Skills:

Place Value—
Tens and Ones

Write the numbers.

4 tens and 6 ones
46

8 tens and 2 ones
_____

2 tens and 5 ones
_____

6 tens and 4 ones
_____

5 tens and 7 ones
_____

1 ten and 8 ones
_____

5 tens and 0 ones
_____

3 tens and 9 ones
_____

If Froggy catches all of the fish that are greater than 50, how many fish will he catch? _____

Frogs

That's Odd!

5 is an odd number.

You can't divide an odd number into groups of two.

Add or subtract.

7 - 3 = _____   5 + 3 = _____

2 + 4 = _____   3 - 0 = _____

6 - 1 = _____   2 + 5 = _____   4 - 2 = _____   9 + 1 = _____

1 - 1 = _____   9 - 3 = _____   8 + 2 = _____   9 - 8 = _____

4 + 5 = _____   5 + 5 = _____   1 + 6 = _____   3 + 6 = _____

8 - 6 = _____   6 - 4 = _____   4 - 4 = _____   7 - 4 = _____

Circle all of the answers that are odd numbers.
Are there more odd answers or even answers?

_____

Frogs

Write the number.

sixteen _____   four hundred _____

eleven _____   twenty-four _____

thirty-three _____   forty-one _____

eighty-one _____   fifty-nine _____

one hundred sixty-five _____   one hundred _____

one hundred twenty-seven _____

two hundred seventy-two _____

*Super Bonus:

One million eight hundred thousand four

_____

Frogs

Freddy's Day

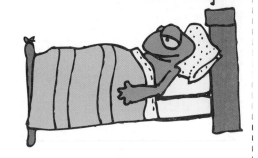

Freddy the Frog wakes up at
7 o'clock in the morning. He
starts catching flies at 9:30 in
the morning. He goes for a swim
at 1 o'clock in the afternoon. He goes to sleep
at 8:30 in the evening.

Which clock shows the time Freddy wakes up?

Which clock shows the time Freddy starts catching flies?

Which clock shows the time Freddy goes for a swim?

Which clock shows the time Freddy goes to sleep?

What time does each clock show?

_____ _____ _____ _____ _____

Frogs

Skills:

Addition and
Subtraction
to 10

Fill in the boxes.

```
  2          7          ☐          7          6
- 0        + ☐        - 3        - 4        - ☐
 ───        ───        ───        ───        ───
  ☐          9          6          ☐          1
```

```
  ☐          8          3          9          ☐
+ 2        - 8        + ☐        - ☐        - 4
 ───        ───        ───        ───        ───
  5          ☐          6          4          1
```

```
  5          2          ☐          8          5
+ 4        + 3        - 5        - 7        + ☐
 ───        ───        ───        ───        ───
  ☐          ☐          5          ☐         10
```

```
 10          3          ☐          5          7
- ☐        + ☐        - 2        - ☐        - 6
 ───        ───        ───        ───        ───
  4          3          4          2          ☐
```

Frogs

TEST YOUR SKILLS

Add and subtract.

7 - 3 = _____   2 + 5 = _____   8 - 6 = _____

5 + 4 = _____   9 - 4 = _____   7 + 3 = _____

Write the numbers.

4 tens and 7 ones _____

3 tens and 4 ones _____

1 ten and 6 ones _____

6 tens and 0 ones _____

Fill in the circle for the missing number.

$\begin{array}{r} 7 \\ + \square \\ \hline 9 \end{array}$
  ○ 3
  ○ 4
  ○ 2
  ○ 5

$\begin{array}{r} \square \\ - 4 \\ \hline 1 \end{array}$
  ○ 5
  ○ 3
  ○ 6
  ○ 7

$\begin{array}{r} \square \\ + 2 \\ \hline 5 \end{array}$
  ○ 2
  ○ 3
  ○ 7
  ○ 4

$\begin{array}{r} 9 \\ - \square \\ \hline 4 \end{array}$
  ○ 5
  ○ 4
  ○ 3
  ○ 2

Read the problem.
Fill in the circle that shows the equation for the problem.

5 frogs were swimming in the pond. 2 more frogs jumped in. How many frogs were in the pond in all?

○ 5 - 2 = 3   ○ 5 + 2 = 7

○ 7 - 5 = 2   ○ 5 + 3 = 2

Write the numbers.

eleven _____   thirty-one _____

eighteen _____   eighty-two _____

twelve _____   sixty-four _____

one hundred twenty-seven _____

Read the problem.

Fill in the circle to answer each question.

Ann wakes up at 7 o'clock in the morning. She goes to school at 8:30. She comes home at 3:30. She goes to bed at 9:00.

What time does Ann wake up?

○   ○   ○   ○

What time does she come home from school?

○   ○   ○   ○

This is a pictograph. It tells about the people who came to the candy store on Saturday. In this graph each picture stands for 2 people.

People Who Came to the Candy Store on Saturday

Women

Men

Boys

Girls

How many women came to the store? _____

How many men came to the store? _____

How many boys came to the store? _____

How many girls came to the store? _____

How many adults came to the store? _____

How many children came to the store? _____

The Candy Store

$$6 + 7 = 13$$

Add.

5 + 6 = _____   3 + 8 = _____   6 + 6 = _____

8 + 8 = _____   7 + 7 = _____   5 + 7 = _____

5 + 8 = _____   9 + 9 = _____   9 + 4 = _____

4 + 7 = _____   7 + 8 = _____   5 + 9 = _____

9 + 2 = _____   6 + 8 = _____   9 + 6 = _____

7 + 6 = _____   7 + 5 = _____   3 + 9 = _____

4 + 8 = _____   9 + 3 = _____   7 + 4 = _____

4 + 9 = _____   2 + 9 = _____   9 + 5 = _____

If a scoop holds no more than 9 jelly beans, what is the largest number of jelly beans that you could have in two scoops? _____ Three scoops? _____

The Candy Store

The candy store is having a sale. Each piece of candy costs 1 cent. Find the total number of candies each child bought.

Rick bought 3 peppermints, 6 lemon drops, and 4 fireballs.

How many candies did he buy in all? _____

How much did he spend? _____

Lydia bought 7 gummy bears, 1 jawbreaker, and 3 caramels.

How many candies did she buy in all? _____

How much did she spend? _____

Laura bought 5 fireballs, 5 gummy bears, and 2 lemon drops.

How many candies did she buy in all? _____

How much did she spend? _____

Gene bought 4 jawbreakers, 2 caramels, and 1 fireball.

How many candies did he buy in all? _____

How much did he spend? _____

The Candy Store

Skills:

Addition Facts to 18

Missing Addends

Add.

$7 + 5 =$ _____ $5 + 6 =$ _____ $9 + 8 =$ _____ $6 + 5 =$ _____

$6 + 8 =$ _____ $8 + 5 =$ _____ $8 + 3 =$ _____ $4 + 7 =$ _____

$4 + 9 =$ _____ $7 + 7 =$ _____ $9 + 2 =$ _____ $8 + 8 =$ _____

$6 + 6 =$ _____ $6 + 7 =$ _____ $6 + 9 =$ _____ $9 + 9 =$ _____

$5 + 9 =$ _____ $8 + 6 =$ _____ $5 + 7 =$ _____ $9 + 4 =$ _____

 $+$  $= 12$  $+$  $= 14$

If ⭐ $= 5$, then ❤ $=$ _____.   If ⬛ $= 6$, then ⬤ $=$ _____.

If ⭐ $= 3$, then ❤ $=$ _____.   If ⬛ $= 7$, then ⬤ $=$ _____.

If ⭐ $= 4$, then ❤ $=$ _____.   If ⬛ $= 9$, then ⬤ $=$ _____.

If ⭐ $= 8$, then ❤ $=$ _____.   If ⬛ $= 8$, then ⬤ $=$ _____.

The Candy Store

18

Rosie bought 18 jelly beans. She gave 9 of them to her brother. How many jelly beans did she keep for herself?

_____

Rudy bought 16 gummy bears. He ate 7 of them and saved the rest for later. How many did he save for later?

_____

Hannah bought
15 fireballs. She took
8 of them to her Brownie meeting to share with her friends. How many fireballs did she have left? _____

Les bought
14 peppermints. He ate
5 and gave the rest to his grandmother. How many peppermints did he give to his grandmother?

_____

Rosa bought
11 jawbreakers. She ate one each day for a week. At the end of the week, how many jawbreakers were left? _____

Write your own problem about candy.

_____

_____

_____

_____

The Candy Store

Skills:

Subtraction
Facts to 18

There were 18 pieces of taffy in the bag. Fred ate 9 pieces. What's left in the bag?

$$18 - 9 = 9$$

14 - 8 = _____   12 - 4 = _____   14 - 6 = _____

13 - 6 = _____   17 - 9 = _____   12 - 7 = _____

15 - 6 = _____   16 - 8 = _____   15 - 7 = _____

11 - 3 = _____   14 - 9 = _____   13 - 7 = _____

15 - 8 = _____   13 - 5 = _____   16 - 7 = _____

13 - 9 = _____   11 - 9 = _____   12 - 6 = _____

14 - 7 = _____   17 - 8 = _____   14 - 5 = _____

The Candy Store

Match each set of coins to the item that costs that amount of money.

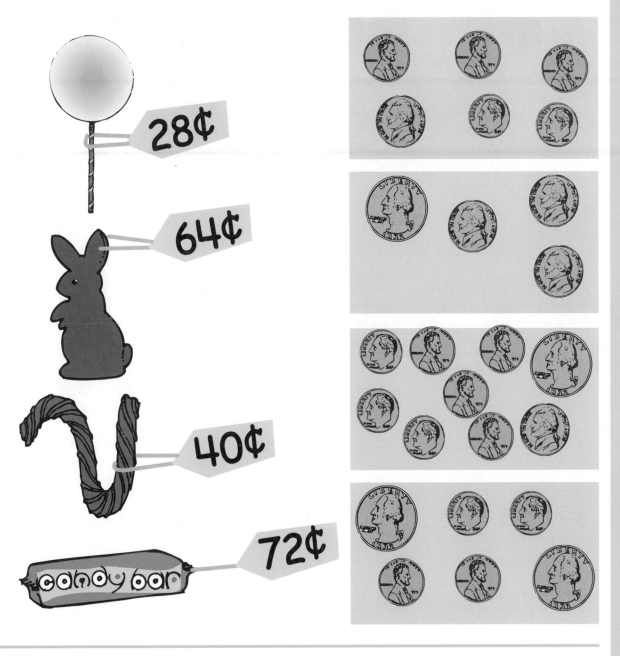

28¢

64¢

40¢

72¢

Show one way to make $1.00 using coins of at least 3 different values. Draw a picture to show your answer.

The Candy Store

The Candy Store

Skills:

Adding Three Numbers

$$3 + 2 + 2 = 7$$

Add.

$2 + 1 + 3 =$ ___ $1 + 4 + 3 =$ ___ $7 + 2 + 0 =$ ___

$4 + 0 + 5 =$ ___ $5 + 0 + 5 =$ ___ $5 + 1 + 4 =$ ___

$6 + 1 + 2 =$ ___ $2 + 2 + 2 =$ ___ $2 + 5 + 2 =$ ___

$5 + 2 + 3 =$ ___ $1 + 5 + 1 =$ ___ $4 + 3 + 1 =$ ___

$3 + 3 + 3 =$ ___ $3 + 1 + 1 =$ ___ $8 + 1 + 1 =$ ___

$2 + 6 + 2 =$ ___ $7 + 2 + 1 =$ ___ $1 + 3 + 3 =$ ___

If 4 boys and 4 girls each had 1 lollipop in each hand, how many lollipops did they have in all? _____

Math • EMC 4547 • © Evan-Moor Corp.

Number facts can be grouped into families.

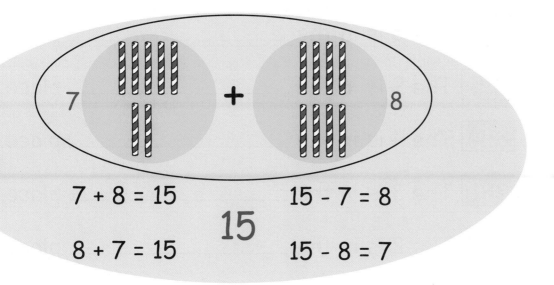

7 + 8 = 15   15 - 7 = 8

15

8 + 7 = 15   15 - 8 = 7

Complete these number families.

5 + 8 = ____	7 + 6 = ____	9 + 5 = ____
8 + 5 = ____	6 + 7 = ____	5 + 9 = ____
13 - 5 = ____	13 - 7 = ____	14 - 9 = ____
13 - 8 = ____	13 - 6 = ____	14 - 5 = ____
7 + 4 = ____	6 + 9 = ____	9 + 4 = ____
4 + 7 = ____	9 + 6 = ____	4 + 9 = ____
11 - 7 = ____	15 - 9 = ____	13 - 4 = ____
11 - 4 = ____	15 - 6 = ____	13 - 9 = ____

The Candy Store

Ones, Tens, Hundreds

Skills:

Place Value—
Hundreds,
Tens, Ones

Money

Write the place value.

235 The 3 is in the _____ place.

915 The 9 is in the _____ place.

854 The 4 is in the _____ place.

361 The 3 is in the _____ place.

782 The 2 is in the _____ place.

159 The 5 is in the _____ place.

796 The 6 is in the _____ place.

473 The 4 is in the _____ place.

Write each amount using the dollar sign.

Example: 2 dollars and 47 cents—$2.47

3 dollars and 11 cents   4 dollars and 95 cents

_____   _____

1 dollar and 84 cents   9 dollars and 60 cents

_____   _____

The Candy Store

Fill in the missing numbers in each number pattern.

156, 157, 158, _____, 160, 161, _____, _____

400, 500, _____, 700, _____, 900

60, 70, 80, _____, 100, 110, _____, _____

15, 20, 25, _____, _____, _____

3, 6, 9, 12, _____, _____, _____

37, 35, 33, 31, _____, 27, _____, _____

55, 65, 75, _____, _____, _____, _____

24, _____, 28, 30, _____, _____

*Extra Challenge:

25, 30, 29, 34, 33, 38, ____, ____, ____, ____

99, 96, 93, ____, ____, ____, ____

The Candy Store

Skills:

Geometric
Shapes

Draw a line from each statement to the correct shape or shapes.

- opposite sides are the same length

- 3 corners

- 4 right angles

- 3 sides

- 4 sides are not all the same length

- 4 sides are the same length

TEST YOUR SKILLS

Robbie bought 5 gumdrops and 9 jelly beans. He ate all the gumdrops and one jelly bean. How many candies are left? _____

Add or subtract.

14 - 7 = ____   6 + 6 = ____   9 - 5 = ____   8 + 4 = ____

9 - ____ = 3   7 + ____ = 11   ____ + 6 = 13   ____ + 7 = 15

Name the place value of each colored numeral.

6**4**2 _____   8**3**6 _____

29 _____   **4**58 _____

Fill in the missing numbers.

15, _____, 21, 24, _____, 30, _____

47, 45, 43, _____, 39, _____, _____

Name each shape.

 _____   _____

Count the money.

                                    _____ ¢

Make It Equal

Group the coins in each box so that the two robots get the same amount of money.

Robots

Skills:

Two-Digit
Addition
Without
Regrouping

First add the **ones**.

```
  35
+ 24
───
   9
```

Then add the **tens**.

```
  35
+ 24
───
  59
```

Add.

14	53	26	60	31
+ 13	+ 10	+ 21	+ 39	+ 17

25	86	41	34	50
+ 32	+ 11	+ 41	+ 55	+ 28

45	66	52	73	81
+ 3	+ 30	+ 26	+ 15	+ 17

Robots

What's a Polygon?

Skills:

Geometric
Shapes

Polygons are shapes
that have straight sides.
They are closed shapes.

These are all polygons.

triangle

square

rectangle

Here are more polygons.

pentagon

hexagon

octagon

How many sides does a hexagon have? _____

What street sign is the shape of an octagon? _____

How many sides does a pentagon have? _____

Draw an **X** through each shape that is **not** a polygon.

Robots

Skills:

Two-Digit
Subtraction
Without
Regrouping

First subtract the **ones**.

$$
\begin{array}{r}
28 \\
-\ 15 \\
\hline
3
\end{array}
$$

Then subtract the **tens**.

$$
\begin{array}{r}
28 \\
-\ 15 \\
\hline
13
\end{array}
$$

Subtract.

73	48	47	26	77
- 50	- 17	- 11	- 20	- 54

85	23	64	39	50
- 42	- 11	- 53	- 16	- 30

55	43	88	69	36
- 13	- 22	- 35	- 47	- 20

Robots

Odd or Even?

Even numbers end in 0, 2, 4, 6, or 8.
Odd numbers end in 1, 3, 5, 7, or 9.
You can find every even number
by counting by twos.

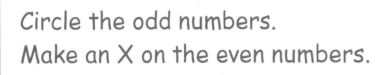

Circle the odd numbers.
Make an X on the even numbers.

17   24   35   40   44   59

Write the next six even numbers.

42, 44, 46, _____, _____, _____, _____, _____, _____

Write the next six odd numbers.

15, 17, 19, _____, _____, _____, _____, _____, _____

Is it odd or even? Circle one.

one dozen	odd	even
your age	odd	even
number of people in your family	odd	even
number of days in a week	odd	even
number of seconds in a minute	odd	even

```
  56
+  7
_____
```
Add the ones.

```
1
  56
+  7
_____
   3
```
Write the 3 ones. Move the ten to the tens place.

```
1
  56
+  7
_____
  63
```
Add the tens.

Add.

```
  24        36        43        57        48
+  8      +  5      +  7      +  4      +  9
```

```
  64        29        75        19        33
+  7      +  1      +  7      +  6      +  9
```

```
  43        52        38        65        76
+  8      +  9      +  7      +  5      +  6
```

Robots

Robot Repairs

Find the answers.

The robots went to the shop for repairs.
Robot K8 needed 17 new bolts.
Robot G04 needed 9 new bolts.
How many more bolts did K8 need?_____

The technicians worked on Robot
S2 for 23 hours. They worked on
Robot YS1 for 8 hours.

How many hours did they work
on these two robots in all?   _____

The technicians checked
35 switches on Robot YS1. They
checked 21 switches on Robot K8.
How many more switches did they
check on Robot YS1?   _____

How many switches did they
check on both robots combined? _____

All the robots got their batteries
recharged. Robot K8 has 5 batteries.
Robot G04 has 9 batteries. Robot
YS1 has 1 battery. Robot S2 has
6 batteries.

How many batteries do the
robots have in all?   _____

Write > or < between
each pair of numbers.

> means greater than
9 > 2

< means less than
1 < 5

14 _____ 27

81 _____ 66

25 _____ 19

36 _____ 42

100 _____ 110

163 _____ 197

435 _____ 316

652 _____ 228

94 _____ 103

Use > or < to make each sentence true.

1. The number of keys on a piano is _____ the
   number of strings on a guitar.

2. The number of days in February is _____ the
   number of days in March.

3. The number of inches in a foot is _____ the
   number of cards in a deck.

Just Regrouping–Subtracting

$$\overset{1\ \ 14}{\cancel{24}}$$
$$-\ 8$$

Regroup to subtract
the ones.

$$\overset{1\ \ 14}{\cancel{24}}$$
$$\underline{-\ 8}$$
$$6$$

Subtract the ones.

$$\overset{1\ \ 14}{\cancel{24}}$$
$$\underline{-\ 8}$$
$$16$$

Subtract the tens.

Subtract.

35	53	91	86	64
− 6	− 9	− 5	− 7	− 8

47	75	22	84	56
− 8	− 7	− 4	− 9	− 8

62	32	90	46	71
− 6	− 8	− 5	− 7	− 8

Robots

On Saturday, the robots went to the beach. Since robots don't like to swim, they decided to be helpful and pick up aluminum cans.

The bar graph below shows how many cans each robot picked up.

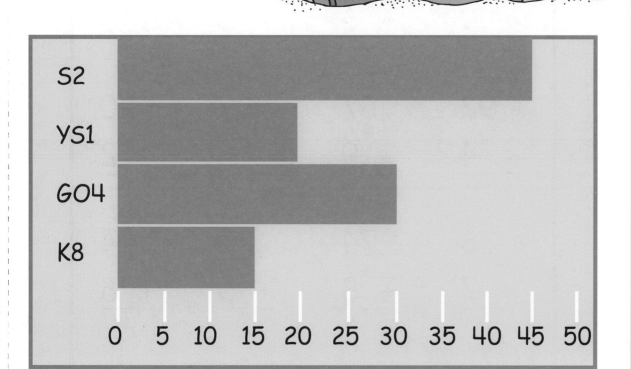

Number of Cans Picked Up

Which robot picked up the most cans? _____

Which robot picked up the fewest cans? _____

How many cans did GO4 pick up? _____

Which robot picked up 20 cans? _____

Robots

Robot Race

Add or subtract. How long will it take you to do these 16 problems? Write the time you begin the robot race.

Starting Time

start

$$48 + 9$$ $$57 + 6$$ $$66 + 5$$ $$75 + 8$$

$$92 - 4$$ $$87 - 9$$ $$63 - 6$$ $$30 - 2$$

$$36 + 7$$ $$74 + 8$$ $$25 + 5$$ $$44 + 6$$

$$45 - 8$$ $$26 - 6$$ $$51 - 4$$ $$25 - 7$$

End

Write down the time the race ended.

This race took _____

Robots

38   UNIT 3

TEST YOUR SKILLS

Fill in the circle for the correct answer.

53 + 13	73 - 50	24 + 8	84 - 9	65 + 9
○ 40	○ 23	○ 24	○ 93	○ 54
○ 60	○ 20	○ 16	○ 75	○ 64
○ 66	○ 32	○ 26	○ 85	○ 74
○ 46	○ 25	○ 32	○ 73	○ 69

Make a match.

hexagon

rectangle

triangle

pentagon

Use > or < to compare the numbers.

14 ◯ 27   100 ◯ 110

81 ◯ 66   123 ◯ 132

25 ◯ 19   436 ◯ 317

55 ◯ 47   652 ◯ 228

31 ◯ 56   994 ◯ 100

Write the next three even numbers.

52, 54, 56, ____, ____, ____

Write the next three odd numbers.

11, 13, 15, ____, ____, ____

Draw an X on the shape that is <u>not</u> a polygon.

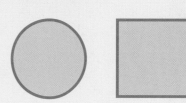

Math on the Farm

Solve each problem two ways—add and multiply.
Show your work.

There are 4 nests in the henhouse. There are 3 eggs in each nest.

How many eggs in all?

There are 2 corrals for the farm horses. There are 5 horses in each corral.

How many horses in all?

There are 3 feeders in the barn. 3 pigs eat at each feeder.

How many pigs in all?

There are 3 geese on the farm. Each goose has 2 babies.

How many baby geese in all?

Farmer John uses tubes to move the water from the big ditch to the small ditches.

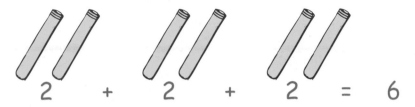

2   +   2   +   2   =   6

How many 2s? _____

3 x 2 = 6

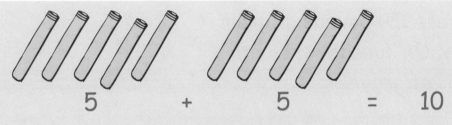

5   +   5   =   10

How many 5s? _____

2 x 5 = 10

Multiply.

2 x 2 = ____   2 x 3 = ____   2 x 4 = ____   2 x 5 = ____

3 x 2 = ____   3 x 3 = ____   3 x 4 = ____   3 x 5 = ____

4 x 2 = ____   4 x 3 = ____   4 x 4 = ____   4 x 5= ____

5 x 2 = ____   5 x 3 = ____   5 x 4 = ____   5 x 5 = ____

On the Farm

How Many? How Much?

Ellie collected 27 eggs on Saturday.
9 of the eggs were white. The rest
of the eggs were brown.

How many eggs were brown? _____

Were there more white eggs or brown eggs? _____

How many more? _____

The cows ate 124 pounds of grain
on Monday. On Tuesday they ate
162 pounds of grain.

On which day did they eat more grain? _____

How much more? _____

Clay and Ellie went for a horseback ride
on Sunday. Ellie rode 12 miles. Clay took
a shortcut and rode only 9 miles.

How many miles did they ride in all? _____

Who rode more miles? _____

How many more? _____

On the Farm

Check these problems. Fill in the squares to show the correct answers. Can Farmer Brown get across his field?

Start

5 x 4 = 9	4 x 2 = 6	5 x 3 = 15	4 x 5 = 9
2 x 2 = 5	1 x 2 = 3	2 x 3 = 6	5 x 2 = 7
3 x 1 = 4	4 x 3 = 15	5 x 4 = 20	2 x 4 = 6
3 x 2 = 5	1 x 4 = 3	3 x 5 = 15	2 x 5 = 12
3 x 4 = 14	5 x 1 = 6	1 x 3 = 3	5 x 5 = 20
4 x 1 = 5	3 x 3 = 6	1 x 5 = 5	4 x 4 = 8

On the Farm

Measure It!

Use a ruler to measure the length of each object pictured. Measure in inches.

_____ inches

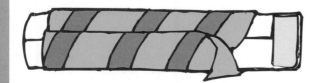

_____ inches

_____ inch

Find something in your house that is about the same length as the pencil. What did you find? _____

Find something in your house that is about the same length as the paper clip. What did you find? _____

Find something in your house that is about the same length as the stick of gum. What did you find? _____

On the Farm

How Many Are Left?

Skills:

Two- and Three-Digit Subtraction with and Without Regrouping

Farmer Jones wants to know how many bags of seed are left after he planted his cornfield.

Solve the problems. Then follow the directions below.

Find each problem with 3 in the tens place. Add those threes.

How many bags of seed are left? _____

33 - 13	96 - 64	85 - 27	47 - 19	68 - 45
467 - 39	665 - 246	438 - 108	543 - 315	582 - 116
377 - 48	524 - 105	176 - 37	266 - 229	413 - 108

On the Farm

About How Many?

Estimate.

Without counting, tell about how many ducks are swimming in the pond. Write your estimate here.

_____

Without counting, tell about how many bees are flying around the hive. Write your estimate here.

_____

Now count to check your answers.

On the Farm

Skills:

Two- and Three-Digit Addition with Regrouping

Place Value

Add.

| 68
+ 14 | 24
+ 28 | 31
+ 9 | 59
+ 27 | 48
+ 36 |

| 142
+ 49 | 249
+ 115 | 729
+ 54 | 817
+ 65 | 408
+ 228 |

| 133
+ 29 | 126
+ 54 | 422
+ 69 | 646
+ 46 | 354
+ 37 |

If the answer has 8 in the tens place, color the egg brown. If the answer has 9 in the tens place, color the egg yellow. If the answer has 6 in the tens place, make the egg spotted.

Count the eggs.

brown _____   yellow _____

white _____   spotted _____

On the Farm

Rounding Off

Clay and Ellie showed their goats at the fair. The judge at the fair asked the children to round off the weight of their goats to the nearest 10 pounds.

Here is the rule for rounding off. If the number in the ones place is **less than 5**, round **down** to the tens place. If the number in the ones place is **5 or greater**, round **up** to the next ten.

Clay's goat weighed 42 pounds.
The number in the ones place is _____.
Is that less than 5? _____ Round down.
42 rounded off to the nearest 10 is 40.

Ellie's goat weighed 48 pounds.
The number in the ones place is _____.
Is that 5 or greater? _____ Round up.
48 rounded off to the nearest 10 is 50.

Round each number to the nearest 10.

62 _____   77 _____   83 _____   51 _____   45 _____

98 _____   22 _____   18 _____   39 _____   12 _____

On the Farm

A Crow's-Eye View

When the crow flew over the pigpens, this is what they looked like. Answer the questions about the shape of each pen.

What is the name of this shape? _____

Is this shape a polygon? _____

How many sides does it have? _____

Are any of the sides equal in length? _____

Are any of the sides parallel? _____

How many corners does it have? _____

Are they square corners? _____

What is the name of this shape? _____

Is this shape a polygon? _____

How many sides does it have? _____

Are any of the sides equal in length? _____

Are any of the sides parallel? _____

How many corners does it have? _____

Are they square corners? _____

What is the name of this shape? _____

Is this shape a polygon? _____

How many sides does it have? _____

Are any of the sides parallel? _____

Are any of the sides equal in length? _____

How many corners does it have? _____

Are they square corners? _____

On the Farm

Counting the Bales

Farmer Jones records the number of hay bales in each of his stacks. He has the numbers for the first and second cuttings. Add the numbers together to see which stack has the most bales.

$$\begin{array}{r} 367 \\ + 128 \\ \hline \end{array} \qquad \begin{array}{r} 224 \\ + 349 \\ \hline \end{array} \qquad \begin{array}{r} 316 \\ + 57 \\ \hline \end{array} \qquad \begin{array}{r} 408 \\ + 366 \\ \hline \end{array} \qquad \begin{array}{r} 149 \\ + 239 \\ \hline \end{array}$$

$$\begin{array}{r} 157 \\ + 628 \\ \hline \end{array} \qquad \begin{array}{r} 906 \\ + 77 \\ \hline \end{array} \qquad \begin{array}{r} 245 \\ + 435 \\ \hline \end{array} \qquad \begin{array}{r} 567 \\ + 239 \\ \hline \end{array} \qquad \begin{array}{r} 626 \\ + 256 \\ \hline \end{array}$$

$$\begin{array}{r} 433 \\ + 248 \\ \hline \end{array} \qquad \begin{array}{r} 628 \\ + 155 \\ \hline \end{array} \qquad \begin{array}{r} 553 \\ + 409 \\ \hline \end{array} \qquad \begin{array}{r} 189 \\ + 112 \\ \hline \end{array} \qquad \begin{array}{r} 365 \\ + 617 \\ \hline \end{array}$$

Circle the stack that has the most bales.

On the Farm

This graph shows how many eggs the hens laid last week. Each square on the graph represents 1 egg.

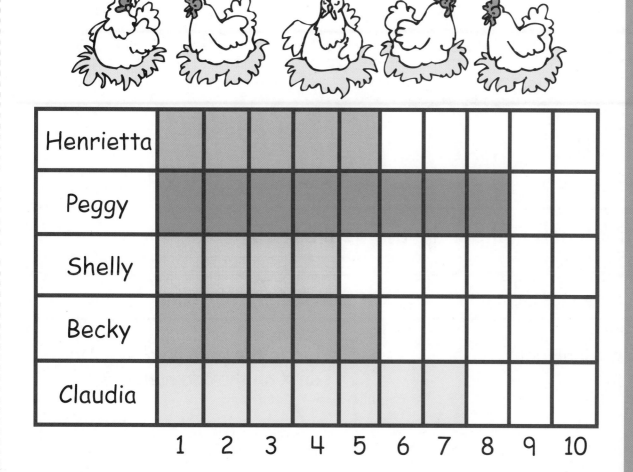

Which hen laid the most eggs? _____Peggy_____

Which hen laid the fewest eggs? _____

How many eggs did Becky lay? _____

How many eggs were laid in all? _____

On the Farm

Add or subtract.

56	157	644	82	463
+ 23	+ 324	- 415	- 24	- 155

Multiply.

3 x 5 = ____   5 x 4 = ____   3 x 3 = ____   4 x 4 = ____

Round each number to the nearest 10.

56 ____   88 ____   14 ____   27 ____   73 ____

Draw a polygon.	Circle the even numbers. Mark an X on the odd numbers.
	17 31 20 56 45 12

Farmer Jones's cows are milked twice a day. Here are his records for Monday and Tuesday.

Monday		Tuesday	
a.m.	43 gallons	a.m.	37 gallons
p.m.	38 gallons	p.m.	47 gallons

On which day was more milk produced? _____

How many more gallons? _____

Find the answers. Draw pictures to help solve each problem.

Luna has 5 rabbits. She gave each rabbit 2 carrots. How many carrots in all?

Doug has 8 mice. He put the mice into 2 cages. He put the same number of mice in each cage.
How many mice in each cage?

Tammy has 5 parrots. She bought 5 peanuts for each parrot to eat.
How many peanuts in all?

Pet Parade

Families of Facts

$$4 \times 2$$
$$8 \div 2$$

$$2 \times 4$$
$$8 \div 4$$

Find the answers to complete each set of related number sentences.

$5 \times 3 = $ _____

$3 \times 5 = $ _____

$15 \div 5 = $ _____

$15 \div 3 = $ _____

$4 \times 5 = $ _____

$5 \times 4 = $ _____

$20 \div 5 = $ _____

$20 \div 4 = $ _____

$3 \times 4 = $ _____

$4 \times 3 = $ _____

$12 \div 4 = $ _____

$12 \div 3 = $ _____

$5 \times 2 = $ _____

$2 \times 5 = $ _____

$10 \div 2 = $ _____

$10 \div 5 = $ _____

Pet Parade

Skills:

Three-Digit Addition with Regrouping

Solve the problems. Color each square that has an answer with 1 in the ones place.

228 + 343	317 + 276	253 + 168	622 + 149
188 + 73	387 + 355	426 + 195	588 + 232
754 + 99	679 + 254	464 + 257	597 + 168
375 + 336	638 + 288	277 + 344	478 + 224

Did you get four in a row? _____

Pet Parade

Ready to Travel

Skills:

Division Facts

Mr. Jones puts pets into transparent boxes for travel. Figure out how many animals go in each box.

How many hamsters? _____

How many boxes? _____

How many hamsters in each box? _____

$$6 \div 2 = 3$$

$9 \div 3 =$ _____

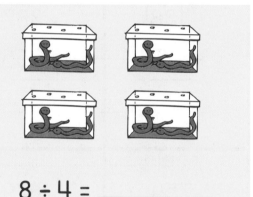

$8 \div 4 =$ _____

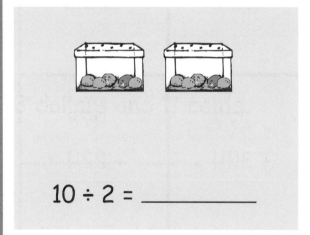

$10 \div 2 =$ _____

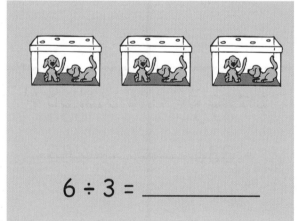

$6 \div 3 =$ _____

$12 \div 3 =$ _____ $15 \div 5 =$ _____ $16 \div 4 =$ _____ $4 \div 2 =$ _____

Skills:

Solving Word
Problems

Solve each problem. Draw a picture to show each answer.

Sherri has 2 dogs. She bought
6 dog biscuits. She gave the
same number of biscuits to each
dog. How many dog biscuits for
each dog?

_____ dog biscuits for each dog

Marshall has 3 cats. He bought
9 toys for the cats. He gave
the same number of toys to
each cat. How many toys for
each cat?

_____ toys for each cat

Jimmy has 12 fish. He put them
in 4 fishbowls. He put the same
number of fish in each bowl.
How many fish in each bowl?

_____ fish in each bowl

Pet Parade

Just Add It!

Skills:

Three-Digit Addition with Regrouping

Pet Parade

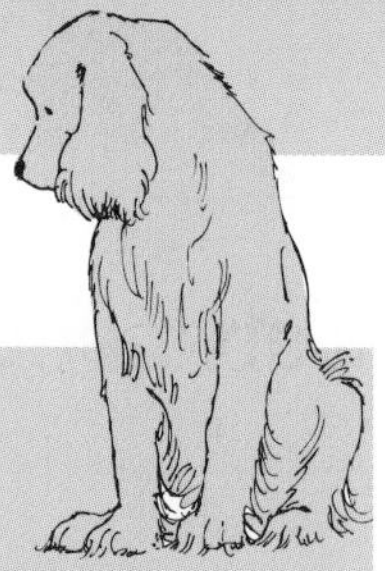

659 + 156	425 + 284	794 + 67	832 + 139
556 + 375	942 + 58	277 + 646	195 + 591
318 + 482	263 + 470	678 + 35	373 + 239
289 + 546	555 + 387	499 + 421	367 + 103

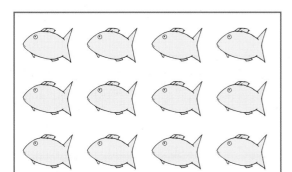

Here are four number sentences that tell about the picture:

$4 \times 3 = 12$ $3 \times 4 = 12$

$12 \div 3 = 4$ $12 \div 4 = 3$

A multiplication sentence is given for each picture. Write a division sentence for each picture.

 $2 \times 3 = 6$

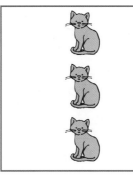 $2 \times 4 = 8$

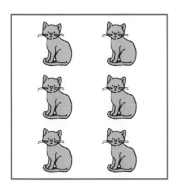 $2 \times 2 = 4$

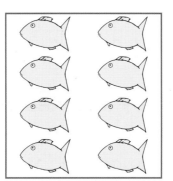 $3 \times 1 = 3$

 $3 \times 5 = 15$

 $3 \times 3 = 9$

Pet Parade

Which Is Better?

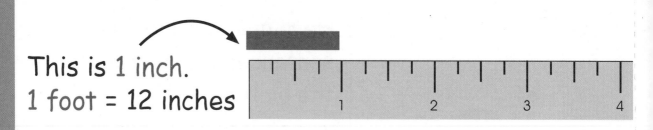

This is 1 inch.
1 foot = 12 inches

Circle the unit of measurement that would be used to measure each of the following items.

1. the height of a tree   inches   feet

2. the width of a book   inches   feet

3. the length of a guinea pig   inches   feet

4. the distance around your waist   inches   feet

5. the height of an elephant   inches   feet

6. the length of a fence   inches   feet

7. the length of a car   inches   feet

8. the height of a cat   inches   feet

9. the distance you can throw a ball   inches   feet

10. the length of your toothbrush   inches   feet

Pet Parade

Perimeter is the distance around a figure. Find the perimeter by adding the measurement given on each side.

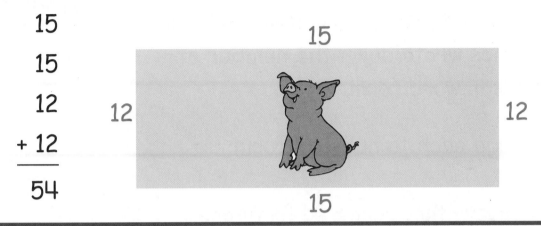

15
15
12
+ 12
———
54

15

12   12

15

Find the perimeter of each pen.

5

5   5

5

The perimeter of the rabbit's pen is _____ feet.

10

10   10

10

The perimeter of the goat's pen is _____ feet.

20

8   8

20

The perimeter of the dog's pen is _____ feet.

Pet Parade

Watch It Run!

The hamster in Doug's cage loves to run in its wheel. The wheel has a clicker that keeps track of each turn. Gramps wrote down the number of turns in word form.

Change each to numeral form.

Monday—three hundred forty-one   _____

Tuesday—six hundred seventy-nine   _____

Wednesday—one hundred thirty   _____

Thursday—five hundred ninety-six   _____

Friday—two hundred fifty   _____

Saturday—four hundred eighty-eight   _____

Sunday—nine hundred   _____

Monday—two hundred sixty-three   _____

Tuesday—three hundred twenty-seven   _____

Wednesday—eight hundred two   _____

Circle the largest number.

Math • EMC 4547 • © Evan-Moor Corp.

Pet Parade

Comparing Numbers

> means greater than
700 > 120

< means less than
20 < 86

Write > or < between each pair of numbers.

72 _____ 44   521 _____ 639

105 _____ 85   74 _____ 73

96 _____ 23   804 _____ 796

89 _____ 37   24 _____ 31

206 _____ 198

Use > or < to make each sentence true.

1. The number of months in a year is _____ the
   number of seasons in a year.

2. The number of seconds in a minute is _____ the
   number of letters in the alphabet.

3. The number of dimes in a dollar is _____ the
   number of pennies in a quarter.

Pet Parade

TEST YOUR
SKILLS

Find the answers to complete each set of number sentences.

$5 \times 3 =$ _____ $\qquad$ $4 \times 3 =$ _____

$3 \times 5 =$ _____ $\qquad$ $3 \times 4 =$ _____

$15 \div 5 =$ _____ $\qquad$ $12 \div 3 =$ _____

$15 \div 3 =$ _____ $\qquad$ $12 \div 4 =$ _____

Add.

228	277	479
+ 343	+ 646	+ 223

195	794	499
+ 591	+ 67	+ 421

This is 1 inch.
1 foot = 12 inches

Fill in the circle for the unit of measurement that would be used to measure each item.

1. height of a tree
   - inches ○
   - feet ○

2. length of a fence
   - inches ○
   - feet ○

3. height of a mouse
   - inches ○
   - feet ○

4. height of an elephant
   - inches ○
   - feet ○

5. distance around your wrist
   - inches ○
   - feet ○

6. distance around a car
   - inches ○
   - feet ○

Fill in the circle for the perimeter of each shape.

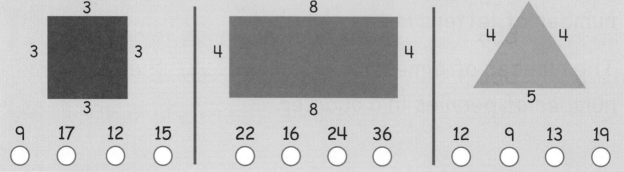

9 ○ 17 ○ 12 ○ 15 ○   22 ○ 16 ○ 24 ○ 36 ○   12 ○ 9 ○ 13 ○ 19 ○

Sink That Putt!

Color the boxes where the problems are solved correctly.
Correct the problems that have been solved incorrectly.

Start here

6 × 1 6	7 × 2 14	8 × 5 35	6 × 3 9	7 × 4 21
8 × 4 28	9 × 4 36	9 × 3 18	6 × 5 11	7 × 7 42
3 × 8 26	8 × 9 72	8 × 6 48	8 × 8 16	9 × 5 40
6 × 9 42	7 × 5 30	3 × 4 12	9 × 6 52	9 × 9 91
8 × 2 18	7 × 6 24	6 × 5 30	7 × 9 56	8 × 1 18
7 × 8 65	5 × 3 8	3 × 7 21	8 × 7 56	6 × 6 36

What a Sport!

Put Them in Order

Numbers that tell about order are called **ordinal numbers**. Use the information in the picture to help you fill in the blanks.

The _____ ball is first in line.

The _____ ball is fifth in line.

The _____ ball is third in line.

The _____ ball is fourth in line.

The _____ ball is second in line.

What is the first day of the week? _____

What is the last month of the year? _____

What is the second letter of your last name? _____

What a Sport!

Home Run

Solve the four problems on each
diamond and score a home run.

Skills:

Addition and
Subtraction with
Regrouping

```
   68
 - 29
```

```
  511
+ 287
```

```
  642
+ 138
```

```
  283
 - 76
```

```
  348
+  93
```

```
  654
 -197
```

```
  445
 -209
```

```
  293
+ 515
```

```
  234
 -164
```

```
  196
 +426
```

```
  921
 -302
```

```
  475
 +  87
```

```
  374
 -175
```

```
  562
 +358
```

```
  366
 +245
```

```
  831
 +159
```

How many runs did you score? _____

What a Sport!

The Sports Report

Prepare the report for the nightly news. Look at the basketball scores below. Fill in the missing information.

| Rexburg Royals | 72 |
| Post Falls Pirates | 59 |

Total points scored _____

_____ won by
_____ points

| Lincoln Loggers | 81 |
| Jackson Jaguars | 67 |

Total points scored _____

_____ won by
_____ points

| Sandpoint Stars | 75 |
| Boise Broncs | 94 |

Total points scored _____

_____ won by
_____ points

| Portland Pioneers | 91 |
| Vancouver Vikings | 66 |

Total points scored _____

_____ won by
_____ points

What a Sport!

Skills:

Estimation

Use estimation to decide if the answer makes sense.

18   80

16   27

There are 16 boys on William's swim team. There are 18 girls. How many swimmers in all?

Answer: about 80 swimmers

Does the answer make sense?

_____ **no** _____

Jose scored 24 points in a basketball game on Friday. He scored 27 points in a basketball game on Saturday. How many points in all?

Answer: about 50 points

Does the answer make sense?

_____

Janine ran for 48 minutes on Monday. On Wednesday she ran for 39 minutes. On Friday she ran for 50 minutes. How many minutes in all?

Answer: about 100 minutes

Does the answer make sense?

_____

Renee spent $4.75 on a ticket to a baseball game. She bought her friend a ticket, too. How much did she spend in all?

Answer: about $10.00

Does the answer make sense?

_____

Matt did 25 push-ups in the morning. He did 51 push-ups in the afternoon. How many push-ups in all?

Answer: about 75 push-ups

Does the answer make sense?

_____

What a Sport!

Dunk the Ball!

Skills:

Multiplication
Facts

Draw a line from each ball to the basket with the correct answer.

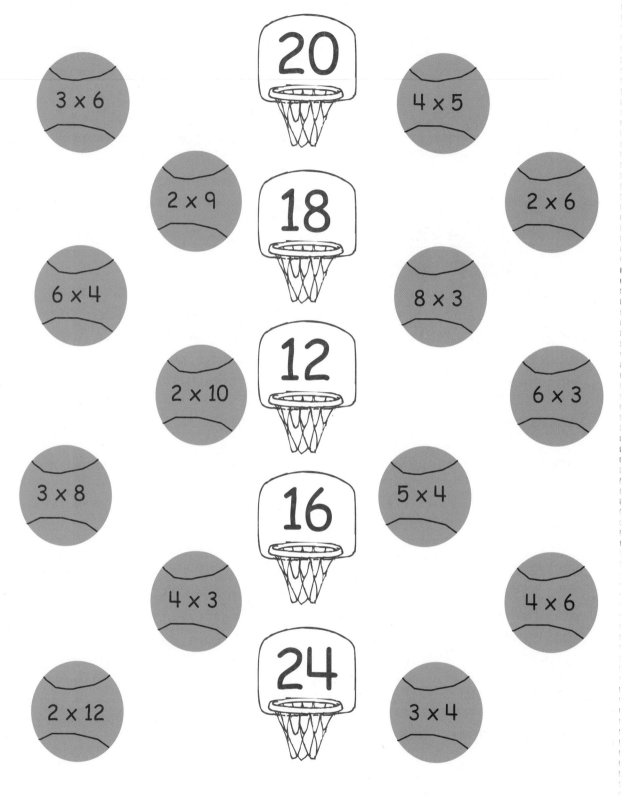

UNIT 6

Math • EMC 4547 • © Evan-Moor Corp.

A **centimeter** (cm) is a unit of measurement. Use the ruler to measure the length of each object pictured.

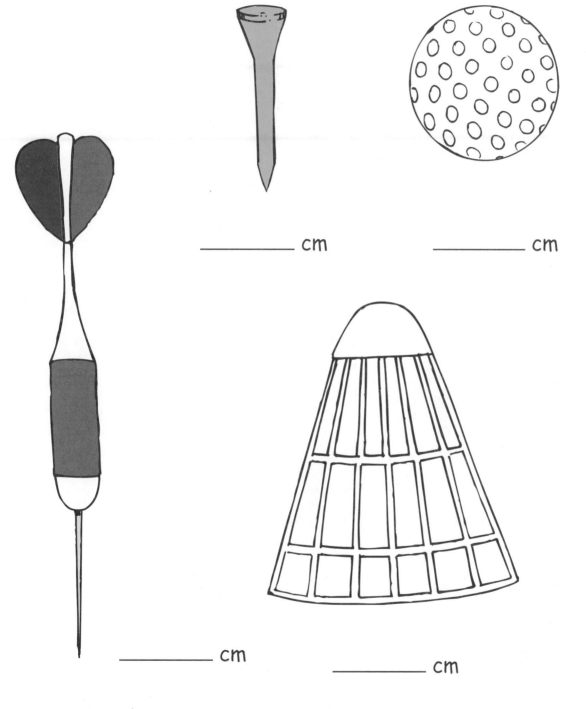

_____ cm   _____ cm

_____ cm   _____ cm

Skills:

Multiplication Facts

Solve each problem to win!

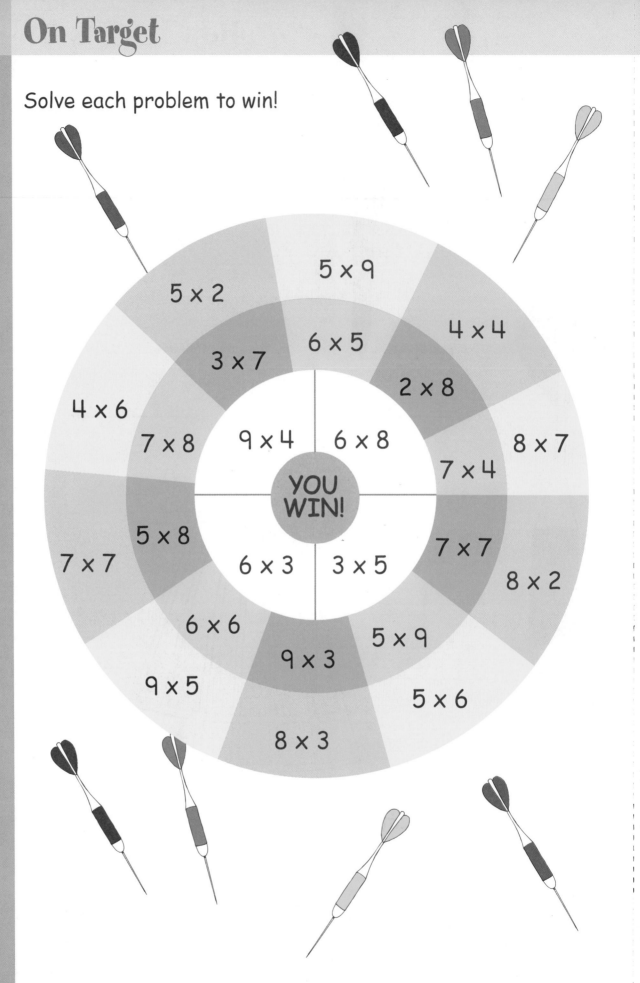

What a Sport!

This is a double bar graph. Notice that there are two bars for each person. Naomi and her friends went bowling. They played two games. The graph below shows their scores.

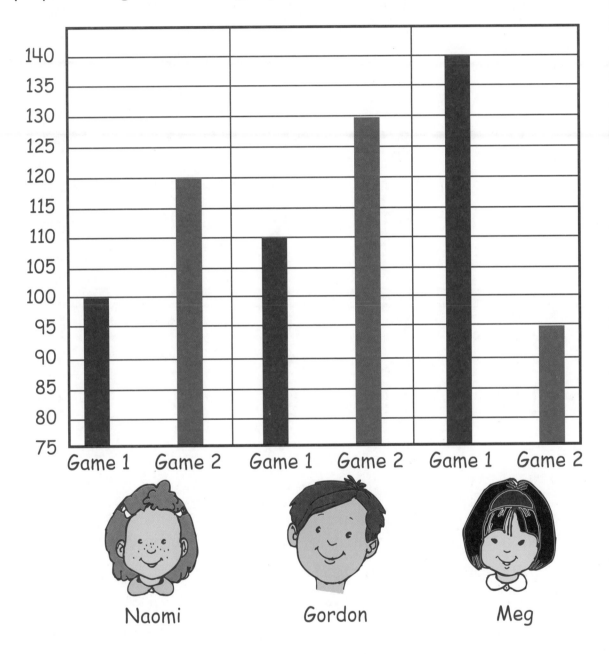

Naomi   Gordon   Meg

How many points are represented by each space on the graph? _____

Which player bowled the highest total for the 2 games? _____

Which player bowled the lowest total for the 2 games? _____

What a Sport!

A Secret Message

Solve each problem.

o	e	i	a	y
52	62	662	91	42
− 31	− 8	− 334	− 35	− 23

b	g	u	n	e
70	168	236	582	795
− 11	− 59	− 207	− 249	− 126

r	r	w	n	i
882	128	357	725	176
− 194	− 79	− 168	− 336	− 88

Start with the letter from the smallest answer. Write the letters in order to the largest answer.

__ __ __ , __ __ __ __ __ __ __

__ __ __ __ __ !

What a Sport!

Skills:

Perimeter

Find the perimeter of each sticker in centimeters.

The perimeter is _____ cm.

The perimeter is _____ cm.

The perimeter is _____ cm.

The perimeter is _____ cm.

The perimeter is _____ cm.

The perimeter is _____ cm.

What a Sport!

Earn a Ticket

Maggie wants to go to the soccer match with the youth center group. A ticket will cost $5.95. Her grandpa tells her she can sell any cans, soda bottles, glass jars, or newspapers she finds in his garage.

1. Maggie found 31 aluminum cans and 22 soda bottles. She got 3 cents for each of the cans and 4 cents for each bottle. How much money did she get?

_____

2. She sold the newspapers by the pound. She gets 9 cents for each of the 30 pounds of newspapers. How much did Maggie get for the newspapers?

_____

3. Finally, she sold a box of old glass jars. She got 7 cents a pound for the glass. The glass weighed 50 pounds. How much money did Maggie get for the glass?

_____

4. What was the total amount of money Maggie got for the bottles, cans, glass, and newspapers?

_____

Can she buy a ticket to the soccer match?

_____

What a Sport!

Solve the problems.

538	256	843	167	422
+ 177	+ 368	- 265	- 89	- 306
☐	☐	☐	☐	☐

Write each number.

Five hundred thirty-nine _____

One hundred ninety-six _____

Seven hundred eight _____

Multiply.

6	7	8	5	9
x 7	x 3	x 6	x 9	x 2
☐	☐	☐	☐	☐

Write the problem. Then solve it.

5 soccer teams took part in a tournament. Three teams had 12 players. Two teams had 11 players. How many players were there in all?

_____

Divide.

$9 \div 3 =$ ___ $12 \div 4 =$ ___ $18 \div 3 =$ ___ $20 \div 5 =$ ___

Skills:

Solving Word
Problems

Once Upon a Time

Multiply or divide to solve each problem. Show your work.

King Crispin is king of
Valoria. 64 flags fly over
King Crispin's castle.
8 flags fly from each
turret. How many turrets
does the castle have?

$64 \div 8 = 8$

The land of Valoria has
8 knights in its service.
Each knight has 4 horses.
How many horses in all?

$8 \times 4 = 32$

King Crispin wants to have a
dinner party. He has 6 tables.
Each table will seat 6 people.
How many people can King
Crispin invite to the party?
Remember that he will need
a chair for himself!

$6 \times 6 = 36 + 1 = 37$

King Crispin's 3 nephews
and 3 nieces came to the
castle for a visit. He was so
happy to see them that he
gave them each 2 gold
coins. How many gold coins
did he give in all?

$2 \times 6 = 12$

Math • EMC 4547 • © Evan-Moor Corp.

King Crispin likes to play croquet. He plays for 2 hours every day, except for Sunday. How many hours does the king play croquet in a week?

$2 + 6 = 12$

King Crispin has 18 falcons. Each of his falconers trains 3 of the birds. How many falconers work for King Crispin?

$18 ÷ 3 = 6$

King Crispin loves to read books. Each week he adds 5 new books to his library. About how many books does he add each month?

$4 × 5 = 20$

The castle's art gallery is shaped like a square. There are 7 paintings on each wall. How many paintings in all?

$7 × 4 = 28$

Once Upon a Time

The Shield of Valoria

Skills:

Multiplication Facts

Odd and Even Numbers

Solve each problem. Color problems with even-numbered answers purple. Color problems with odd-numbered answers orange.

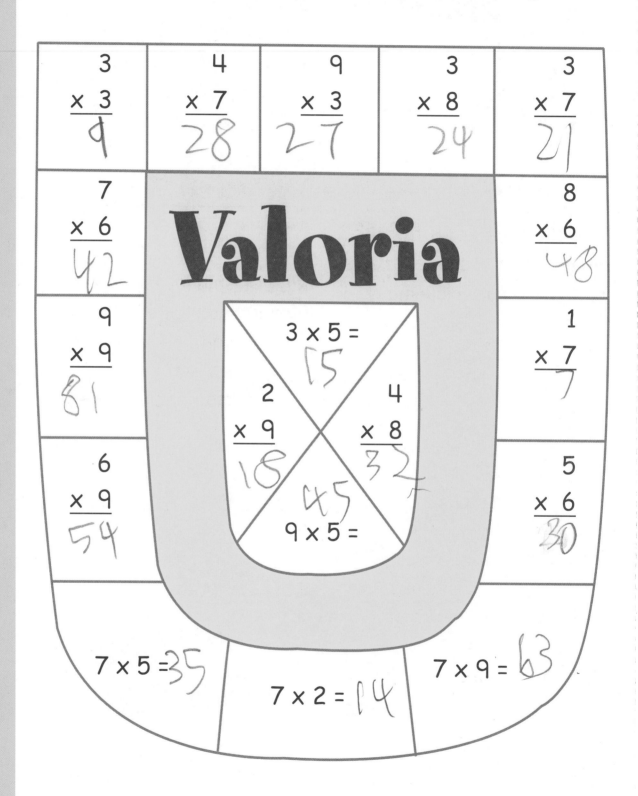

$$3 \times 3 = 9$$
$$4 \times 7 = 28$$
$$9 \times 3 = 27$$
$$3 \times 8 = 24$$
$$3 \times 7 = 21$$
$$7 \times 6 = 42$$
$$8 \times 6 = 48$$
$$9 \times 9 = 81$$
$$1 \times 7 = 7$$
$$6 \times 9 = 54$$
$$5 \times 6 = 30$$

Valoria

$$3 \times 5 = 15$$
$$2 \times 9 = 18$$
$$4 \times 8 = 32$$
$$9 \times 5 = 45$$

$$7 \times 5 = 35$$
$$7 \times 2 = 14$$
$$7 \times 9 = 63$$

Once Upon a Time

80

UNIT 7

Math • EMC 4547 • © Evan-Moor Corp.

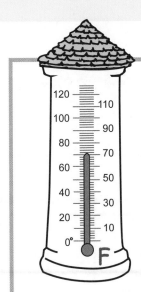

A thermometer is used to measure temperature. Some thermometers use the Fahrenheit scale.

On most thermometers, each space counts for 2 degrees. This thermometer shows 72 degrees Fahrenheit.

72°F

On the Fahrenheit scale, water freezes at 32°.

Water boils at 212°.

What temperature does each thermometer show? Circle to tell whether each temperature shown is cold or warm.

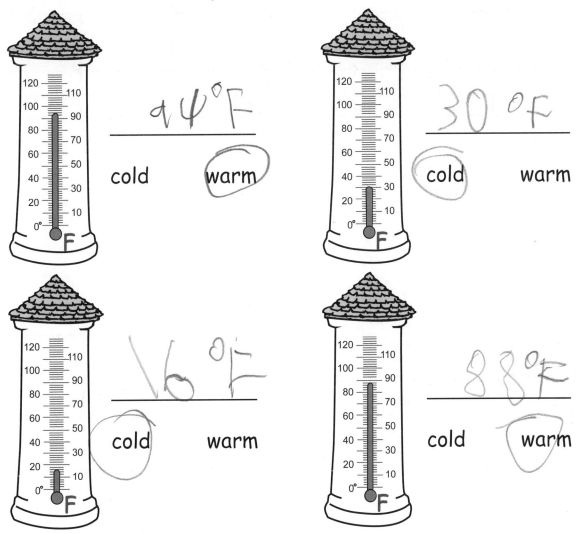

94°F

cold   (warm)

30°F

(cold)   warm

16°F

(cold)   warm

88°F

cold   (warm)

Skills:

Reading a Graph

Once Upon a Time

This graph shows Valoria's rainfall in inches for the past year.

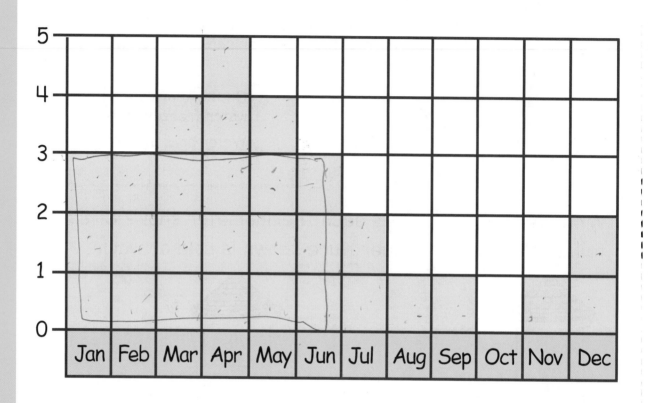

Which month had the greatest rainfall? _____Apr_____

In which month was there no rain at all? _____Oct_____

Which three-month period had the greatest amount of rainfall? _____May Mar_____

What season occurs during that time period? _____spring_____

What was the total rainfall for the year? _____29 inches_____

Skills:

Division Facts

Solve each of the problems to build a strong wall.
How quickly can you do it?

$2 \div 2 =$ 1	$24 \div 3 =$ 8	$5 \div 5 =$ 1
$4 \div 2 =$ 2	$27 \div 3 =$ 9	$10 \div 5 =$ 2

$6 \div 2 =$ 3	$3 \div 3 =$ 1		$4 \div 4 =$ 1	$15 \div 5 =$ 3
$8 \div 2 =$ 4	$6 \div 3 =$ 2	$32 \div 4 =$ 8	$8 \div 4 =$ 2	$20 \div 5 =$ 4
$10 \div 2 =$ 5	$9 \div 3 =$ 3	$36 \div 4 =$ 9	$12 \div 4 =$ 3	$25 \div 5 =$ 5
$12 \div 2 =$ 6	$12 \div 3 =$ 4		$16 \div 4 =$ 4	$30 \div 5 =$ 6
$14 \div 2 =$ 7	$15 \div 3 =$ 5		$20 \div 4 =$ 5	$35 \div 5 =$ 7
$16 \div 2 =$ 8	$18 \div 3 =$ 6		$24 \div 4 =$ 6	$40 \div 5 =$ 8
$18 \div 2 =$ 9	$21 \div 3 =$ 7		$28 \div 4 =$ 7	$45 \div 5 =$ 9

Once Upon a Time

Marble Walkways

King Crispin is having some walkways built in his garden. The walkways are made of square marble tiles. Each tile measures 1 foot on each side.

King Crispin wants to know the area of each section of walkway. **Area** is measured in square units. One way to find the area is to count the units. The area of this section of walkway is 6 square feet.

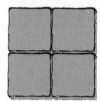

Find the area of each section.

The area of this section of

walkway is _____ square feet.

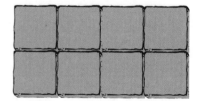

The area of this section of

walkway is _____ square feet.

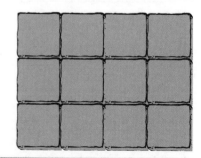

The area of this section of

walkway is _____ square feet.

Can you think of another way to find the area of each section

besides counting? _____

Connect the dots in order. Count by 2s.

Once Upon a Time

Skills:

Multiplication and Division Facts

Greater Than, Less Than

Once Upon a Time

Each pennant represents a knight. King Crispin's pennant is yellow. Solve the problems and color the pennants to find him.

Make the pennant:

green if the answer is greater than 10 and less than 50

red if the answer is greater than 2 and less than 10

yellow if the answer is greater than 50 and less than 70

Multiply or divide.

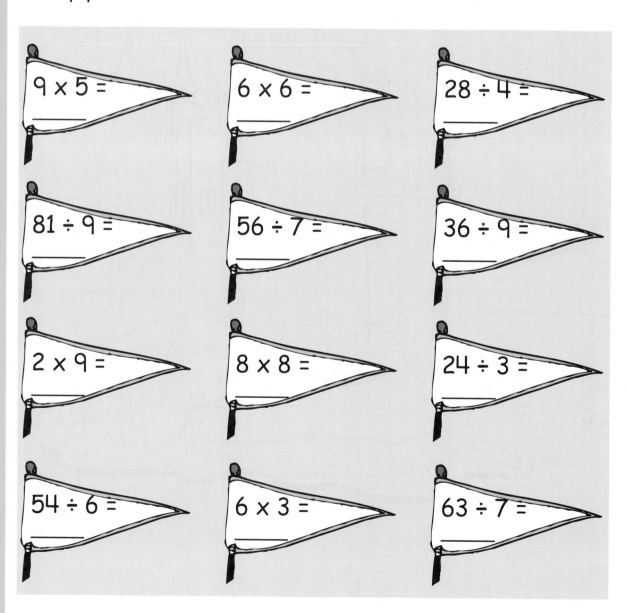

$9 \times 5 =$ ___

$6 \times 6 =$ ___

$28 \div 4 =$ ___

$81 \div 9 =$ ___

$56 \div 7 =$ ___

$36 \div 9 =$ ___

$2 \times 9 =$ ___

$8 \times 8 =$ ___

$24 \div 3 =$ ___

$54 \div 6 =$ ___

$6 \times 3 =$ ___

$63 \div 7 =$ ___

Skills:

Three-Digit
Addition and
Subtraction
with and
Without
Regrouping

Add or subtract.

$$\begin{array}{r} \$7.46 \\ + 1.46 \\ \hline \end{array} \qquad \begin{array}{r} 254 \\ + 263 \\ \hline \end{array} \qquad \begin{array}{r} 815 \\ + 178 \\ \hline \end{array}$$

$$\begin{array}{r} 523 \\ - 145 \\ \hline \end{array} \qquad \begin{array}{r} \$4.71 \\ + 2.78 \\ \hline \end{array} \qquad \begin{array}{r} 333 \\ - 94 \\ \hline \end{array} \qquad \begin{array}{r} 685 \\ - 367 \\ \hline \end{array} \qquad \begin{array}{r} 832 \\ - 466 \\ \hline \end{array}$$

$$\begin{array}{r} 243 \\ + 380 \\ \hline \end{array} \qquad \begin{array}{r} 465 \\ + 199 \\ \hline \end{array} \qquad \begin{array}{r} 559 \\ + 376 \\ \hline \end{array} \qquad \begin{array}{r} 806 \\ + 154 \\ \hline \end{array} \qquad \begin{array}{r} \$1.16 \\ + 2.34 \\ \hline \end{array}$$

$$\begin{array}{r} 667 \\ - 355 \\ \hline \end{array} \qquad \begin{array}{r} 846 \\ - 159 \\ \hline \end{array} \qquad \begin{array}{r} \$3.20 \\ + 1.32 \\ \hline \end{array} \qquad \begin{array}{r} 705 \\ - 417 \\ \hline \end{array} \qquad \begin{array}{r} 168 \\ + 645 \\ \hline \end{array}$$

Once Upon a Time

The King's Hat

Plot each point on the grid.
Connect the points as you find them.

1. (3, 4)	5. (5, 9)	9. (9, 9)	13. (11, 4)
2. (2, 6)	6. (6, 8)	10. (10, 7)	14. (3, 4)
3. (3, 8)	7. (7, 10)	11. (11, 8)	
4. (4, 7)	8. (8, 8)	12. (12, 6)	

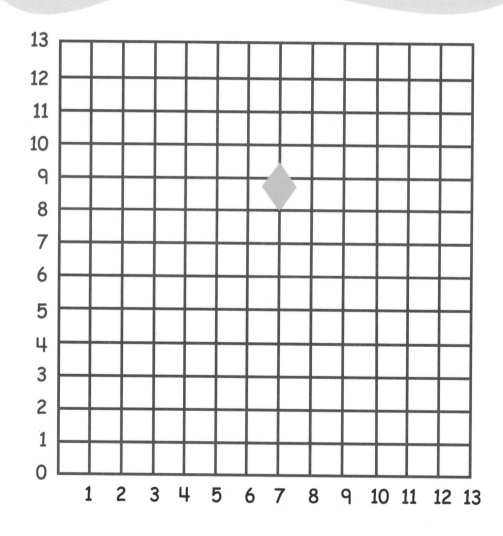

Is the king's hat symmetrical?   yes   no

Once Upon a Time

TEST YOUR SKILLS

Add or subtract.

$6.47
+ 2.35
_____

815
+ 178
_____

523
- 145
_____

$3.30
- 1.22
_____

846
- 159
_____

243
+ 380
_____

Multiply. Fill in the circle.

4 x 8 = _____
Ⓐ 40   Ⓒ 32
Ⓑ 24   Ⓓ 12

7 x 8 = _____
Ⓐ 65   Ⓒ 48
Ⓑ 56   Ⓓ 15

9 x 5 = _____
Ⓐ 45   Ⓒ 72
Ⓑ 36   Ⓓ 56

8 x 6 = _____
Ⓐ 14   Ⓒ 48
Ⓑ 32   Ⓓ 50

Divide. Fill in the circle.

6 ÷ 3 = _____
Ⓐ 2   Ⓒ 9
Ⓑ 3   Ⓓ 18

12 ÷ 4 = _____
Ⓐ 5   Ⓒ 3
Ⓑ 4   Ⓓ 6

32 ÷ 4 = _____
Ⓐ 8   Ⓒ 6
Ⓑ 4   Ⓓ 3

25 ÷ 5 = _____
Ⓐ 6   Ⓒ 5
Ⓑ 9   Ⓓ 7

Find the area. ☐ = 1 square foot

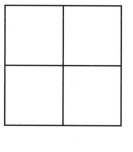

_____ square feet

_____ square feet

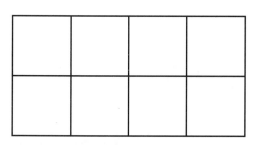

_____ square feet

Multiply or divide to solve each problem.

The queen had 6 children. She gave each child 3 gold coins. How many gold coins did she give in all?

_____ gold coins

The king had 15 horses. He gave each of his sons 5 horses. How many sons did the king have?

_____ sons

Count by 2s.

2 4 ___ ___ ___ 14 ___ ___ ___ 22 ___ ___ ___ ___

Treasure Below

Skills:

Multiplication
Facts

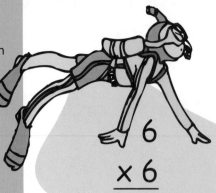

Solve each problem. Connect answers
with **3** in the tens place.

$$\begin{array}{r} 6 \\ \times 6 \\ \hline \end{array}$$ $$\begin{array}{r} 8 \\ \times 8 \\ \hline \end{array}$$ $$\begin{array}{r} 6 \\ \times 4 \\ \hline \end{array}$$ $$\begin{array}{r} 8 \\ \times 3 \\ \hline \end{array}$$

$$\begin{array}{r} 9 \\ \times 7 \\ \hline \end{array}$$ $$\begin{array}{r} 9 \\ \times 4 \\ \hline \end{array}$$ $$\begin{array}{r} 7 \\ \times 8 \\ \hline \end{array}$$ $$\begin{array}{r} 9 \\ \times 9 \\ \hline \end{array}$$

$$\begin{array}{r} 9 \\ \times 6 \\ \hline \end{array}$$ $$\begin{array}{r} 6 \\ \times 7 \\ \hline \end{array}$$ $$\begin{array}{r} 5 \\ \times 6 \\ \hline \end{array}$$ $$\begin{array}{r} 6 \\ \times 8 \\ \hline \end{array}$$

$$\begin{array}{r} 3 \\ \times 9 \\ \hline \end{array}$$ $$\begin{array}{r} 8 \\ \times 5 \\ \hline \end{array}$$ $$\begin{array}{r} 9 \\ \times 5 \\ \hline \end{array}$$ $$\begin{array}{r} 7 \\ \times 5 \\ \hline \end{array}$$

$$\begin{array}{r} 7 \\ \times 7 \\ \hline \end{array}$$ $$\begin{array}{r} 9 \\ \times 8 \\ \hline \end{array}$$ $$\begin{array}{r} 6 \\ \times 8 \\ \hline \end{array}$$ $$\begin{array}{r} 4 \\ \times 9 \\ \hline \end{array}$$

Under the Sea

The weight of each fish can be measured using the units **pounds** and **ounces**.

1 pound = 16 ounces

Circle the heavier fish in each box.

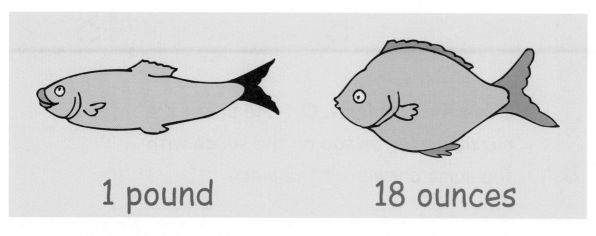

1 pound   18 ounces

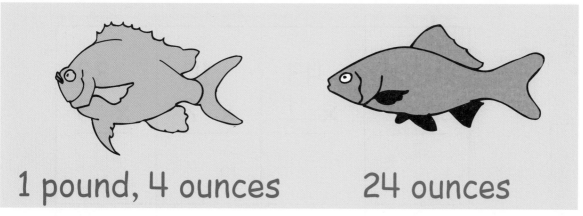

1 pound, 4 ounces   24 ounces

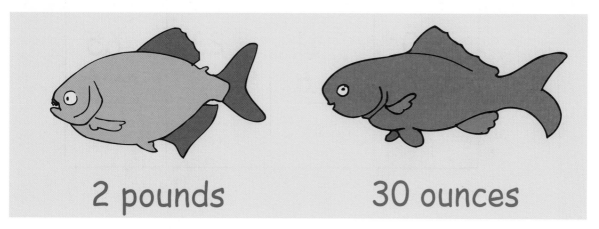

2 pounds   30 ounces

Under the Sea

Skills: Multiplication Without Regrouping

Multiply bigger numbers.

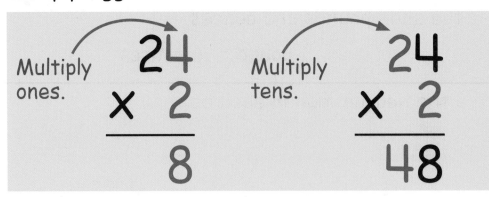

Multiply ones.   24
              × 2
              ———
                8

Multiply tens.   24
              × 2
              ———
               48

Solve the problems. Cut and paste the puzzle pieces on top of the space with the same answer as the piece.

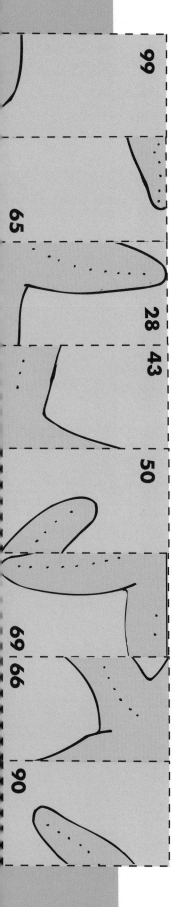

25 × 2	43 × 1	14 × 2	33 × 3
10 × 9	11 × 6	23 × 3	65 × 1

Skills:

Solving Word
Problems

Max and Maria are deep-sea divers. They study the underwater animals.

Solve each problem. Label each answer.

Max found a sunken ship. He found 7 piles of coins around the ship. There were 30 coins in each pile. How many coins did Max find?

_____

Maria saw 11 octopuses. How many tentacles (arms) in all?

_____

Max counted 23 lobsters. Each lobster had 2 claws. How many claws in all?

_____

Maria collected oysters, clams, and scallops. She collected 21 of each. How many shellfish did she collect in all?

_____

Under the Sea

More Diving

Maria is wearing 2 oxygen tanks. Each tank holds enough oxygen for 40 minutes of diving. How much diving time does she have in all?

_____

Max has an underwater camera. He has taken 2 rolls of pictures. Each roll has 24 pictures. How many pictures has he taken in all?

_____

Maria saw 5 schools of fish. There were 30 fish in each school. How many fish in all?

_____

Last year Max went diving 2 days each week during every week of the year. How many days did Max go diving last year?

_____

The campers at Seaside Adventure Camp have many activities to choose from. This graph shows the activities enjoyed on one Friday. This kind of graph is called a **circle graph**.

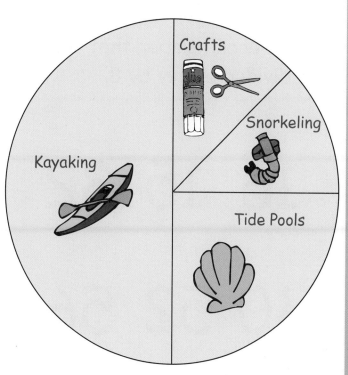

What fraction of the campers went kayaking?

_____

What fraction of the campers went to the tide pools?

_____

Did more campers snorkel or kayak? _____

Did more campers do crafts or go to the tide pools?

_____

If there are 32 campers at Seaside Adventure Camp, how many campers took part in each activity?

kayaking _____   tide pools _____

crafts _____   snorkeling _____

Under the Sea

Divide It Evenly

Circle each number that can be divided evenly by 8.

16 15 32

40 52 56

Circle each number that can be divided evenly by 5.

5 10 23

35 45 39

Solve the problems. Color the fish.

If the answer is 1 through 125, make the fish orange.

If the answer is 126 through 200, make the fish purple.

If the answer is 201 through 300, make the fish green.

Skills:

Multiplication Facts

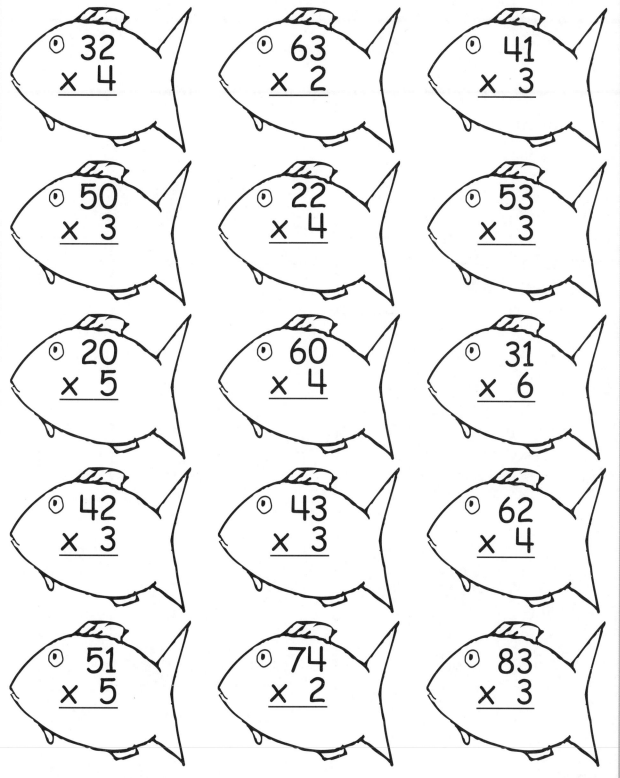

$$\begin{array}{r} 32 \\ \times\ 4 \\ \hline \end{array}$$

$$\begin{array}{r} 63 \\ \times\ 2 \\ \hline \end{array}$$

$$\begin{array}{r} 41 \\ \times\ 3 \\ \hline \end{array}$$

$$\begin{array}{r} 50 \\ \times\ 3 \\ \hline \end{array}$$

$$\begin{array}{r} 22 \\ \times\ 4 \\ \hline \end{array}$$

$$\begin{array}{r} 53 \\ \times\ 3 \\ \hline \end{array}$$

$$\begin{array}{r} 20 \\ \times\ 5 \\ \hline \end{array}$$

$$\begin{array}{r} 60 \\ \times\ 4 \\ \hline \end{array}$$

$$\begin{array}{r} 31 \\ \times\ 6 \\ \hline \end{array}$$

$$\begin{array}{r} 42 \\ \times\ 3 \\ \hline \end{array}$$

$$\begin{array}{r} 43 \\ \times\ 3 \\ \hline \end{array}$$

$$\begin{array}{r} 62 \\ \times\ 4 \\ \hline \end{array}$$

$$\begin{array}{r} 51 \\ \times\ 5 \\ \hline \end{array}$$

$$\begin{array}{r} 74 \\ \times\ 2 \\ \hline \end{array}$$

$$\begin{array}{r} 83 \\ \times\ 3 \\ \hline \end{array}$$

Under the Sea

Skills:

Fraction of a
Set of Objects

Sometimes fractions tell about parts of a group.
$\frac{1}{2}$ of the shells are yellow.

Write a fraction to show the number of yellow shells in each group.

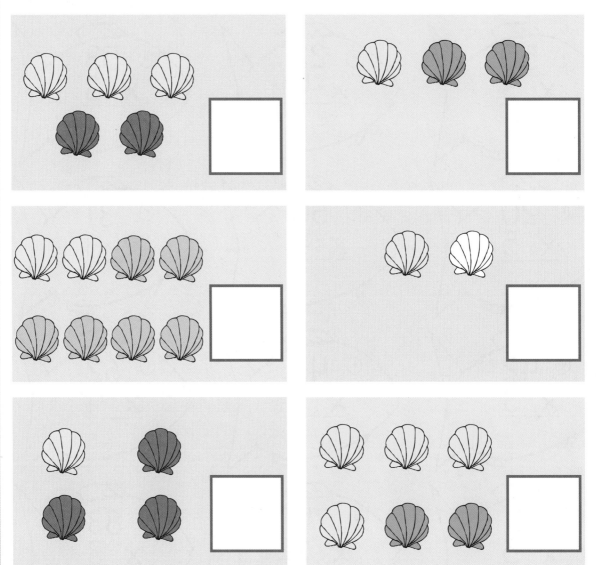

Math • EMC 4547 • © Evan-Moor Corp.

Under the Sea

Skills:

Multiplication
with Regrouping

Regrouping in Multiplication

① Multiply ones.
$3 \times 4 = 12$

② Write 2 in the
ones place.

③ Write the ten in
the tens place.

④ Multiply tens.
$3 \times 2 = 6$

Add the regrouped ten.
$6 + 1 = 7$

③ 1
24
× 3 ①
————
④ **72** ②

Write the correct answer in each pearl to claim it.

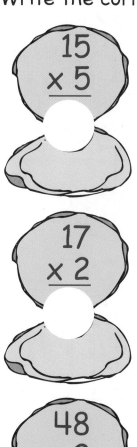

15
× 5

26
× 3

34
× 4

17
× 2

45
× 3

22
× 6

48
× 2

51
× 5

36
× 2

Under the sea

Equivalent Fractions

$\frac{1}{2}$ of this shape is blue. 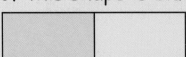 $\frac{2}{4}$ of this shape is blue.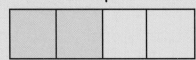

$\frac{1}{2} = \frac{2}{4}$. These are **equivalent fractions.**

Match the sets of equivalent fractions.

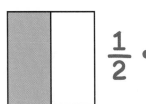 $\frac{1}{2}$ •

•$\frac{2}{8}$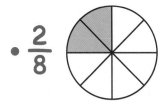

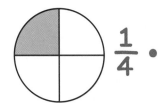 $\frac{1}{4}$ •

•$\frac{6}{8}$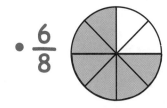

$\frac{2}{3}$ •

•$\frac{2}{4}$

$\frac{3}{4}$ •

•$\frac{4}{6}$

Math • EMC 4547 • © Evan-Moor Corp.

Skills:

Symmetry

Some figures can be cut or folded along a line so that both sides match.

This line is called a **line of symmetry**. It divides the figure so that both sides are exactly the same. The figure is **symmetrical**.

Circle the shells that are exactly the same on both sides. Make an **X** on the shells that are <u>not</u> the same.

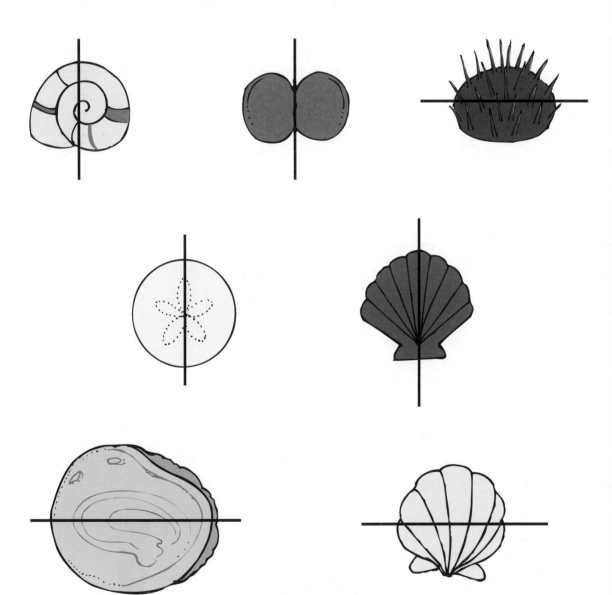

Under the Sea

TEST YOUR SKILLS

Multiply or divide.

3 x 7 = _____   9 x 9 = _____   6 x 8 = _____   8 x 3 = _____   5 x 6 = _____

54 ÷ 9 = _____   72 ÷ 9 = _____   40 ÷ 5 = _____   36 ÷ 6 = _____   28 ÷ 4 = _____

Multiply.

$$\begin{array}{r} 34 \\ \times\ 2 \\ \hline \end{array}$$ 　　$$\begin{array}{r} 46 \\ \times\ 1 \\ \hline \end{array}$$ 　　$$\begin{array}{r} 23 \\ \times\ 4 \\ \hline \end{array}$$ 　　$$\begin{array}{r} 11 \\ \times\ 5 \\ \hline \end{array}$$ 　　$$\begin{array}{r} 37 \\ \times\ 3 \\ \hline \end{array}$$

Color each shape to show the fraction given.

$\frac{1}{2}$ 　　　　　$\frac{1}{4}$ 　　　　　$\frac{2}{3}$

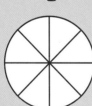 　　  　　

Circle each shape that has a line of symmetry.

 　　 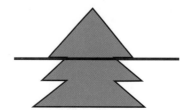 　　

Skills:

Multiplication
Without
Regrouping

Multiply.

$$
\begin{array}{r}
131 \\
\times\ \ 3 \\
\hline
\end{array}
\qquad
\begin{array}{r}
220 \\
\times\ \ 3 \\
\hline
\end{array}
\qquad
\begin{array}{r}
314 \\
\times\ \ 2 \\
\hline
\end{array}
\qquad
\begin{array}{r}
121 \\
\times\ \ 4 \\
\hline
\end{array}
$$

$$
\begin{array}{r}
403 \\
\times\ \ 2 \\
\hline
\end{array}
\qquad
\begin{array}{r}
203 \\
\times\ \ 3 \\
\hline
\end{array}
\qquad
\begin{array}{r}
343 \\
\times\ \ 2 \\
\hline
\end{array}
\qquad
\begin{array}{r}
211 \\
\times\ \ 3 \\
\hline
\end{array}
$$

$$
\begin{array}{r}
104 \\
\times\ \ 2 \\
\hline
\end{array}
\qquad
\begin{array}{r}
424 \\
\times\ \ 2 \\
\hline
\end{array}
\qquad
\begin{array}{r}
421 \\
\times\ \ 2 \\
\hline
\end{array}
\qquad
\begin{array}{r}
432 \\
\times\ \ 2 \\
\hline
\end{array}
$$

Write each answer from above in the correct train car.

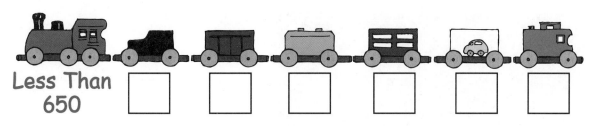

Less Than
650

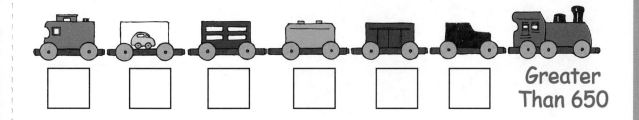

Greater
Than 650

On the Go

Out in Space

Skills:

Three-Dimensional Shapes

Objects with these shapes have special names.

This is a cube:

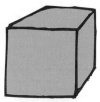

This is a sphere:

This is a cone:

This is a cylinder:

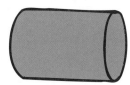

Write the name of each shape.

_____

_____

_____

_____

On the Go

Math • EMC 4547 • © Evan-Moor Corp.

Skills:

Multiplication
with Regrouping

Multiply.

$$\overset{1\ 2}{137} \times 3$$
411

$$238 \times 2$$

$$206 \times 4$$

$$119 \times 5$$

$$146 \times 2$$

$$223 \times 4$$

$$328 \times 3$$

$$225 \times 2$$

$$134 \times 2$$

$$102 \times 5$$

$$425 \times 2$$

$$317 \times 3$$

$$126 \times 4$$

$$245 \times 2$$

$$139 \times 2$$

On the Go

Plot the coordinates in order on the grid. Connect the points as you find them.

1. (3, 2)	7. (2, 7)	13. (6, 7)	19. (11, 7)
2. (3, 5)	8. (1, 8)	14. (7, 6)	20. (11, 5)
3. (6, 5)	9. (2, 9)	15. (8, 5)	21. (12, 5)
4. (5, 6)	10. (3, 9)	16. (8, 7)	22. (12, 2)
5. (4, 7)	11. (4, 9)	17. (9, 7)	23. (10, 2)
6. (3, 8)	12. (5, 8)	18. (10, 7)	24. (5, 2)
			25. (3, 2)

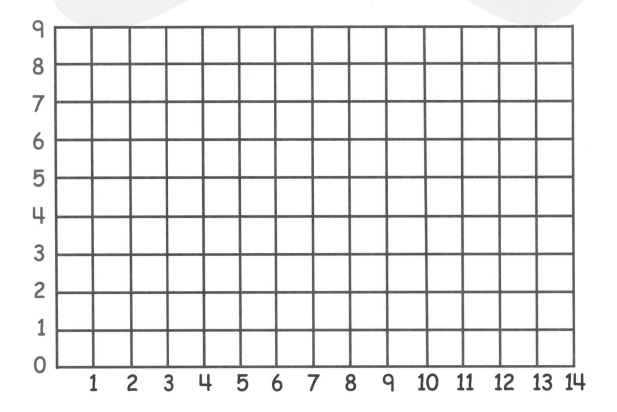

Add details to this rescue vehicle.

Solve each problem to move through the maze.

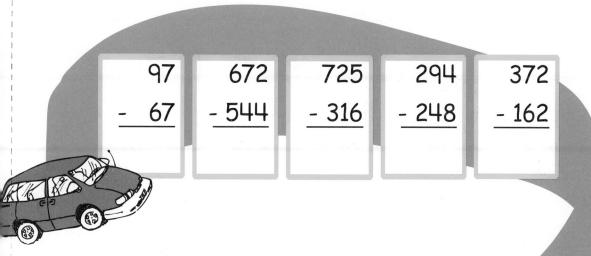

97	672	725	294	372
− 67	− 544	− 316	− 248	− 162

581	468	285	860	347
− 264	− 173	− 279	− 62	− 135

356	535	167	740	633
− 174	− 246	− 98	− 351	− 418

WIN!

On the Go

Make a Graph

The children in Mr. Carlile's class come to school in a variety of ways. Color the circle graph to show the following information.

$\frac{1}{4}$ of the children ride in cars (blue)

$\frac{3}{8}$ of the children ride the bus (red)

$\frac{1}{8}$ of the children walk (yellow)

$\frac{1}{4}$ of the children ride bicycles (green)

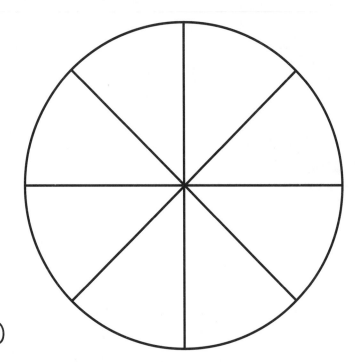

There are 24 children in the class.

How many children walk to school? _____

How many children ride their bikes? _____

How many children ride the bus? _____

HINT: The graph is divided into 8 equal parts; $24 \div 8 =$ ☐,

so each section of the graph represents _____ children.

On the Go

Skills:

Division Facts

Find the answers. Show your work.

32 tires

How many cars? _____

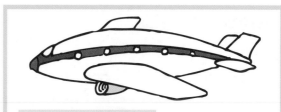

18 wings

How many planes? _____

27 tires

How many trikes? _____

16 sails

How many boats? _____

14 wheels

28 wheels

How many skateboards?

_____

How many bikes? _____

On the Go

A Riddle

Solve the problems. Use each answer to find a letter in the key. Write the letters in order at the bottom of the page.

Multiply or divide.

start →

$6\overline{)24}$ $9\overline{)63}$ $7\overline{)35}$ $7\overline{)42}$

$8\overline{)64}$ $9 \times 4 =$ $6 \times 6 =$ $9\overline{)81}$

$7\overline{)7}$ $6\overline{)36}$ $6\overline{)12}$ $4\overline{)32}$

$5\overline{)30}$ $12 \times 3 =$ $2 \times 5 =$ $4 \times 6 =$

$4 \times 3 =$ $6\overline{)6}$ $9\overline{)72}$ $7 \times 9 =$

$5\overline{)25}$ $9\overline{)36}$ $3 \times 8 =$ $5 \times 5 =$

When is a car not a car?

___ ___ ___ ___   ___ ___   ___ ___ ___ ___ ___   ___ ___ ___ ___

___   ___ ___ ___ ___ ___ ___ ___ ___ ___

w = 4	s = 2	e = 5	y = 25	i = 8	d = 12	u = 9
r = 1	h = 7	o = 10	n = 6	v = 63	t = 36	a = 24

Skills:

Division Facts

Tell how many passengers in each vehicle.

81 passengers

9 planes

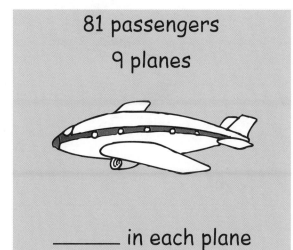

_____ in each plane

60 passengers

3 buses

_____ in each bus

48 passengers

8 cars

_____ in each car

15 passengers

5 helicopters

_____ in each helicopter

72 passengers

8 vans

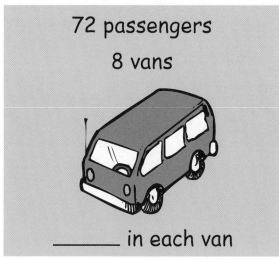

_____ in each van

49 passengers

7 boats

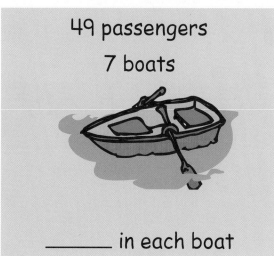

_____ in each boat

On the Go

What's Afloat?

Connect the dots.

▲ Count by 2s.

■ Count by 3s.

● Count by 4s.

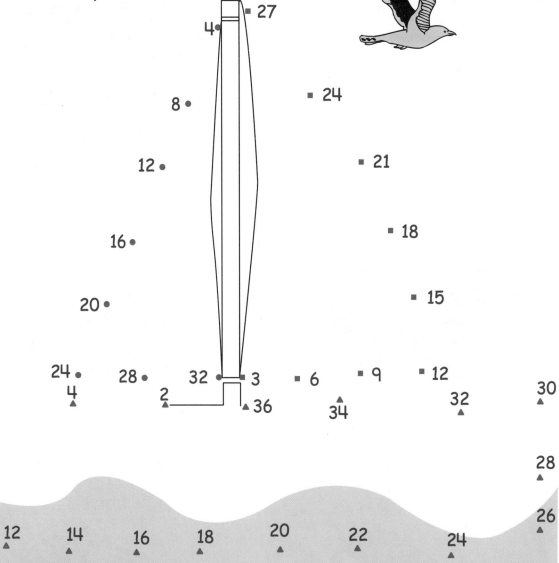

Skills:

Fractions

Some of the packages in each group are special delivery. They must be delivered by 10 a.m. Help the delivery person spot the special packages.

Read the fraction. Color the correct number of packages red.

SPECIAL DELIVERY $\frac{1}{2}$

SPECIAL DELIVERY $\frac{2}{3}$

SPECIAL DELIVERY $\frac{3}{5}$

SPECIAL DELIVERY $\frac{3}{4}$

On the Go

TEST YOUR SKILLS

Multiply. You may need to regroup.

220	343	224	203
x 2	x 3	x 3	x 3

Circle the numbers that are less than 550.

643   545   700

265   556   485

Multiply or divide.

$6\overline{)24}$ 9 x 4 = ____ $7\overline{)35}$

6 x 6 = ____ $6\overline{)12}$ $9\overline{)72}$

3 x 8 = ___ $9\overline{)36}$ 4 x 3 = ___

Fill in the circle for the correct answer.

12 wheels How many bikes?	32 tires How many cars?
Ⓐ 4 Ⓒ 3 Ⓑ 8 Ⓓ 6	Ⓐ 6 Ⓒ 8 Ⓑ 7 Ⓓ 10
15 tires How many trikes?	8 wheels How many wagons?
Ⓐ 3 Ⓒ 4 Ⓑ 5 Ⓓ 2	Ⓐ 3 Ⓒ 5 Ⓑ 2 Ⓓ 4

Subtract. You may need to regroup.

581	468	285	740	633	860
- 264	- 173	- 279	- 351	- 418	- 34

Read each fraction. Fill in the correct number of dots.

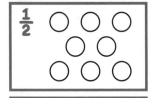

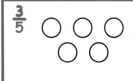

Match.

 •   • cylinder

 •   • cube

 •   • cone

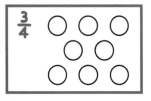

Skills:
Division with
Remainders

Sometimes a number can **not** be divided evenly. For example, I have 7 books to put on 2 shelves. I want to put the same number on each shelf.

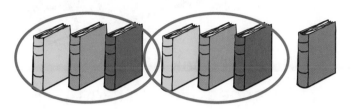

$$2\overline{)7}\quad\frac{3\ r\ 1}{}$$
$$\frac{-\ 6}{1}$$

Three books go on a shelf. There is one extra book. This is called a **remainder**.

Each shelf must have the same number of books. How many books can go on each shelf? Will there be any extra books?

1. 19 books, 2 shelves

   __9__ books on a shelf,

   __1__ extra

2. 58 books, 6 shelves

   _____ books on a shelf,

   _____ extra

3. 24 books, 5 shelves

   _____ books on a shelf,

   _____ extra

4. 75 books, 9 shelves

   _____ books on a shelf,

   _____ extra

Work Space

$$2\overline{)19}\quad\frac{9\ r\ 1}{}$$
$$\frac{-\ 18}{1}$$

On the Bookshelf

Be a Bookworm

Multiply or divide to solve each problem.
Label each answer.

Letitia read 36 pages each day for a week. How many pages did Letitia read in all?

_____

Roger's book has 87 pages. He can read 9 pages an hour. Will it take him more than 9 hours to finish the book?

_____

Barb read 4 books every week during her summer vacation. Her vacation lasted 10 weeks. How many books did Barb read?

_____

Lisa read for 5 hours last week. She read about 40 pages per hour. About how many pages did she read in all?

_____

Skills:

Solving Word Problems

Larry read 6 books of poetry. Each book had 38 poems. How many poems did Larry read in all?

_____

Dennis volunteered in the library on Saturday, shelving books. He worked for 3 hours. He put 96 books on the shelves. How many books did he put away each hour?

_____

Juanita read about elephants for 25 minutes. She read 5 articles. About how many minutes did it take Juanita to read each article?

_____

Bobby read a mystery book with 7 chapters. The book was 67 pages long. Did all the chapters have the same number of pages?

_____

On the Bookshelf

Stack Them, Please

Mrs. Paul, the librarian, wants the books put into stacks of 8 books each! How many books will be left?

On the Bookshelf

47 books $$\begin{array}{r} 5 \\ 8{\overline{)47}} \\ 40 \\ \hline 7 \end{array}$$ _____5_____ stacks _____7_____ books left	**89 books** _____ stacks _____ books left
59 books _____ stacks _____ books left	**42 books** _____ stacks _____ books left
35 books _____ stacks _____ books left	**72 books** _____ stacks _____ books left

UNIT 10

Math • EMC 4547 • © Evan-Moor Corp.

Rita likes to read. She keeps track of the books she has read on the graph below.

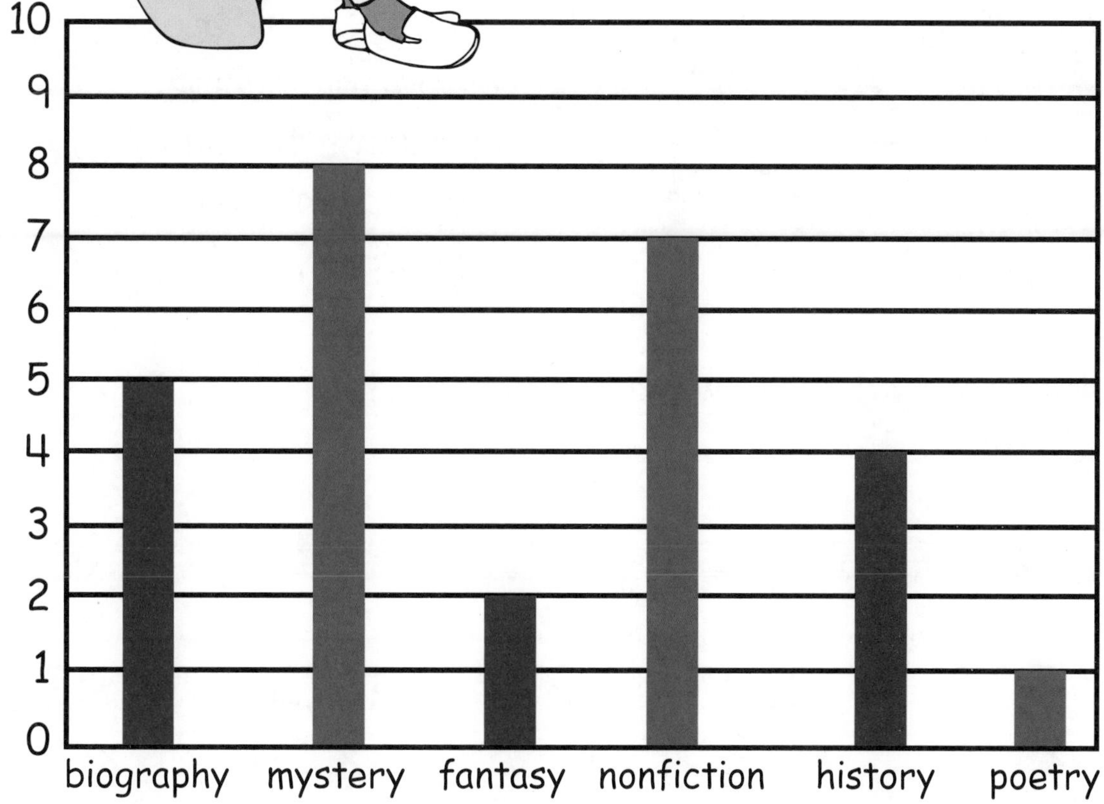

	biography	mystery	fantasy	nonfiction	history	poetry
10						
9						
8		8				
7				7		
6						
5	5					
4					4	
3						
2			2			
1						1
0						

On the Bookshelf

Which kind of book does Rita like best? _____

Has Rita read more mystery books or more poetry books? _____

How many more? _____

Has Rita read more fantasy books or more nonfiction books? _____

How many more? _____

How many biography and history books has Rita read in all? _____

How many books has Rita read in all? _____

Skills:

Multiplication with Regrouping

On the Bookshelf

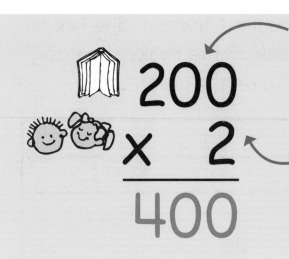

The top number in each problem represents the number of pages read.

The bottom number represents the number of students who read that many pages.

Multiply to find out how many pages each group of students read.

a	b	c	d	e
500	262	371	116	427
× 3	× 2	× 3	× 4	× 2

f	g	h	i	j
315	603	426	511	138
× 5	× 4	× 3	× 5	× 2

Which group read the most? _____

UNIT 10

Draw a line from each set of coins to the comic book with that price.

$1.25

95¢

99¢

$1.00

On the Bookshelf

A Colorful Collection

Skills:

Division with and Without Remainders

Divide to solve each problem. Then color the books.

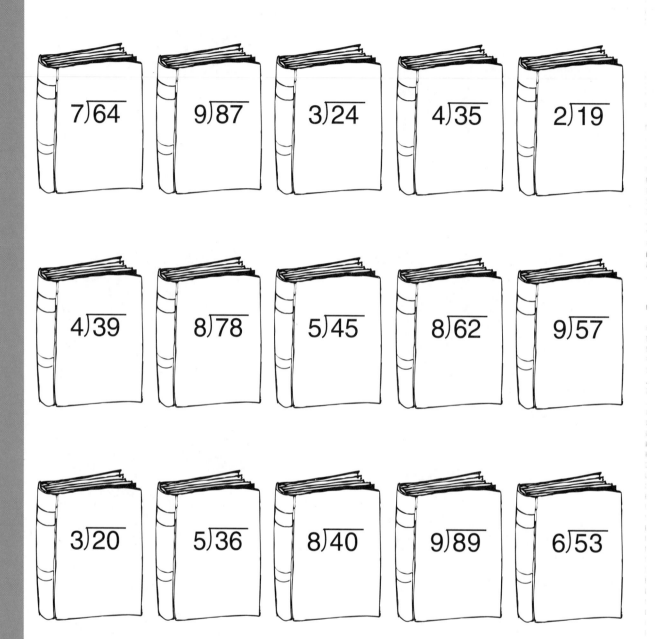

$7\overline{)64}$ $9\overline{)87}$ $3\overline{)24}$ $4\overline{)35}$ $2\overline{)19}$

$4\overline{)39}$ $8\overline{)78}$ $5\overline{)45}$ $8\overline{)62}$ $9\overline{)57}$

$3\overline{)20}$ $5\overline{)36}$ $8\overline{)40}$ $9\overline{)89}$ $6\overline{)53}$

Remainders of 1—Color the book yellow.

Remainders of more than 1—Color the book red.

No remainder—Color the book blue.

On the Bookshelf

Skills:
Congruency

Find the shape in each row that matches the shape at the beginning of the row.

On the Bookshelf

A New Bookcase

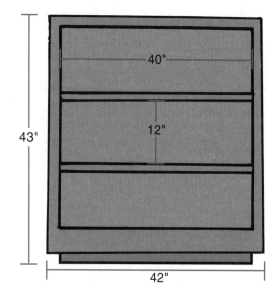

Mrs. Sample built this new bookcase for her books.

How tall is the bookcase? _____

How wide is the bookcase? _____

What is the perimeter of the bookcase? _____

If Mrs. Sample has a set of 12 books and each book is 2 inches wide, will the set fit on one shelf? _____

If Mrs. Sample's atlas is 24 inches tall, will it fit on a shelf? _____

Skills:

Number Words

Write each number.

Four thousand three hundred sixty-four _____

One thousand one hundred twelve _____

Six thousand two hundred one _____

Eight thousand fifty _____

Three thousand six hundred seventy-five _____

Four thousand eight hundred twenty-two _____

Seven thousand ninety-three _____

One thousand five hundred thirty-seven _____

Nine thousand one hundred eighty-nine _____

One thousand seven hundred forty-eight _____

Six thousand four _____

Eight thousand nine hundred sixteen _____

On the Bookshelf

Fractions

Each shelf holds 10 books. Some of the books are checked out. Write a fraction that tells what part of each shelf's books are checked out.

On the Bookshelf

_____

_____

_____

_____

_____

UNIT 10

Math • EMC 4547 • © Evan-Moor Corp.

Multiply.

421	215	326	239	400
x 2	x 4	x 3	x 2	x 4

Divide.

$7\overline{)59}$ $6\overline{)40}$ $5\overline{)43}$ $8\overline{)67}$ $9\overline{)75}$

Write the fraction that names the shaded part of each group.

_____   _____

Write the name of each shape.

_____   _____   _____

Add or subtract.

777	356	597	813
- 189	+ 208	+ 164	- 467

TEST YOUR SKILLS

How much money?

     _____

Bayview School had an aluminum can recycling contest. Room 7 brought in 26 pounds of cans each day for 5 days. Room 10 brought in 15 pounds of cans the first day and 30 pounds each day on the remaining 4 days.

How many pounds of cans were collected?

Room 7 _____ pounds   Room 10 _____ pounds

Give the perimeter.

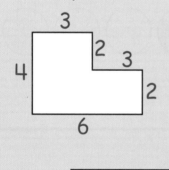

_____

What place is the 8 in?

85   _____

8,257   _____

18   _____

831   _____

Read the graph.
Answer the questions.

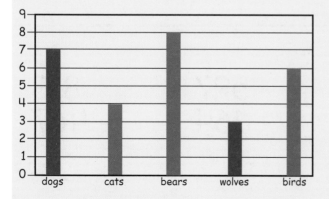

Sam loved to read stories about animals. How many different animals did she read about?

_____

Did she read more books about cats and wolves together or bears?

_____

How many books about four-legged animals did she read in all?

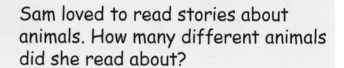

_____

Tracking Form

Topic	Color in each page you complete.						
Frogs	3	4	5	6	7	8	9
	10	11	12	13	14		
The Candy Store	15	16	17	18	19	20	21
	22	23	24	25	26	27	
Robots	28	29	30	31	32	33	34
	35	36	37	38	39		
On the Farm	40	41	42	43	44	45	46
	47	48	49	50	51	52	
Pet Parade	53	54	55	56	57	58	59
	60	61	62	63	64		
What a Sport!	65	66	67	68	69	70	71
	72	73	74	75	76	77	
Once Upon a Time	78	79	80	81	82	83	84
	85	86	87	88	89		
Under the Sea	90	91	92	93	94	95	96
	97	98	99	100	101	102	
On the Go	103	104	105	106	107	108	109
	110	111	112	113	114		
On the Bookshelf	115	116	117	118	119	120	121
	122	123	124	125	126	127	128

Red numbers indicate Test Your Skills pages.

Math • EMC 4547 • © Evan-Moor Corp.

Answer Key

Page 3

How Many Frogs?

There are __4__ red frogs.
There are __2__ green frogs.
How many red and green frogs in all? __6__
Do you add or subtract? __add__

Show your work.
$4 + 2 = 6$

There is __1__ big red frog.
There are __3__ small red frogs.
How many more small red frogs? __2__
Do you add or subtract? __subtract__

Show your work.
$3 - 1 = 2$

How many yellow frogs? __3__
How many red frogs? __4__
How many green frogs? __2__
How many frogs in all? __9__
Do you add or subtract? __add__

Show your work.
$3 + 4 + 2 = 9$

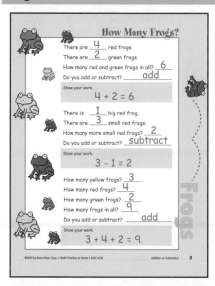

Page 4

Hopping Home

Help find frog. Add. Color the lily pads of 8 or more green.
Start here.

$5 + 3 = $ **8**
$4 + 3 = $ 7
$6 + 1 = $ 7
$3 + 0 = $ 3
$2 + 7 = $ **9**
$1 + 4 = $ 5
$0 + 0 = $ 0
$3 + 2 = $ 5
$7 + 1 = $ **8**
$3 + 5 = $ **8**
$6 + 0 = $ 6
$3 + 3 = $ 6
$4 + 2 = $ 6
$7 + 3 = $ **10**
$3 + 3 = $ 6
$3 + 4 = $ 7
$4 + 5 = $ **9**
$2 + 6 = $ **8**
$8 + 1 = $ **9**
$9 + 1 = $ **10**

Page 5

Frog Fun

Choose the number sentence that fits each story.

4 frogs were swimming in the pond. 3 more frogs jumped in. How many frogs in the pond in all?
$4 - 3 = 1$
$4 + 3 = 7$
$7 - 4 = 3$

A big yellow frog ate 6 flies. A small red frog ate 5 flies. How many more flies did the yellow frog eat?
$5 - 0 = 5$
$6 + 5 = 11$
$6 - 5 = 1$

Draw a picture to show each answer.

6 frogs were sitting on a log. 3 frogs hopped off. How many frogs were left on the log?

5 frogs were croaking a happy tune. 2 more frogs joined in. How many frogs were singing in all?

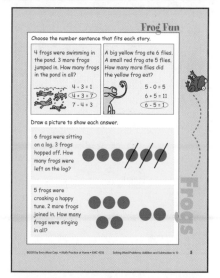

Page 6

Tasty Flies

How many flies did frog eat?

$8 + 1 = $ 9
$5 + 1 = $ 6
$3 + 5 = $ 8
$6 + 2 = $ 8
$6 + 4 = $ 10
$0 + 7 = $ 7
$0 + 8 = $ 8
$8 + 2 = $ 10
$6 + 3 = $ 9
$4 + 3 = $ 7
$1 + 5 = $ 6
$5 + 5 = $ 10
$7 + 3 = $ 10
$2 + 2 = $ 4
$1 + 3 = $ 4
$5 + 4 = $ 9
$2 + 5 = $ 7
$4 + 2 = $ 6
$3 + 3 = $ 6
$3 + 6 = $ 9

*Super Bonus: How many flies did frog eat in all? __153__

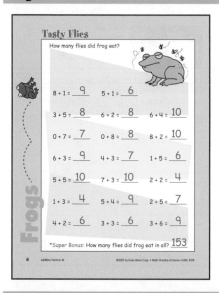

Page 7

Pond Sweet Pond

Graphs show facts and give information. This is a pictograph. It uses pictures to give information. Each picture stands for 1 animal.

Animals Who Live in the Pond
Frogs
Turtles
Snakes
Fish

How many frogs live in the pond? __8__
How many turtles live in the pond? __4__
How many snakes live in the pond? __2__
Are there more frogs or more turtles? __frogs__
How many more? __4__
Are there more turtles or more snakes? __turtles__
How many more? __2__
Are there more fish or more frogs? __frogs__
How many more? __2__

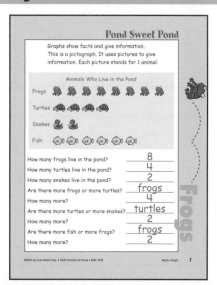

Page 8

How Many Are Left?

4 frogs   4
- 2 frogs   - 2
  2 frogs   2

Subtract.

$5 - 3 = 2$ $10 - 9 = 1$ $3 - 3 = 0$ $9 - 4 = 5$ $8 - 2 = 6$
$8 - 4 = 4$ $10 - 7 = 3$ $6 - 5 = 1$ $5 - 1 = 4$ $6 - 6 = 0$
$9 - 3 = 6$ $8 - 5 = 3$ $9 - 6 = 3$ $10 - 5 = 5$ $7 - 5 = 2$
$2 - 0 = 2$ $4 - 3 = 1$ $5 - 4 = 1$ $6 - 3 = 3$ $7 - 2 = 5$

Page 9

Froggy Fishes

Write the numbers.

4 tens and 6 ones __46__
8 tens and 2 ones __82__
2 tens and 5 ones __25__
6 tens and 4 ones __64__
5 tens and 7 ones __57__
1 ten and 8 ones __18__
5 tens and 0 ones __50__
3 tens and 9 ones __39__

If Froggy catches each of the fish that is greater than 50, how many fish will he catch? __3__

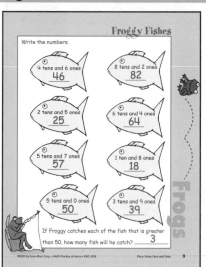

Page 10

That's Odd!

5 is an odd number.
You can't divide an odd number into groups of two.

Add or subtract.

$7 - 3 = 4$ $5 + 3 = 8$
$2 + 4 = 6$ $3 - 0 = ③$
$6 - 1 = ⑤$ $2 + 5 = ⑦$ $4 - 2 = 2$ $9 + 1 = 10$
$1 - 1 = 0$ $9 - 3 = 6$ $8 + 2 = 10$ $9 - 8 = ①$
$4 + 5 = ⑨$ $5 + 5 = 10$ $1 + 6 = ⑦$ $3 + 6 = ⑨$
$8 - 6 = 2$ $6 - 4 = 2$ $4 - 4 = 0$ $7 - 4 = ③$

Circle all of the answers that are odd numbers.
Are there more odd answers or even answers?
__More even (4 more even)__

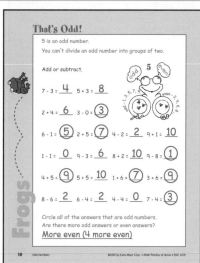

Page 11

What Does It Say?

Write the number.

sixteen __16__
four hundred __400__
eleven __11__
twenty-four __24__
thirty-three __33__
forty-one __41__
eighty-one __81__
fifty-nine __59__
one hundred sixty-five __165__
one hundred __100__
one hundred twenty-seven __127__
two hundred seventy-two __272__

*Super Bonus:
One million eight hundred thousand four
__1,800,004__

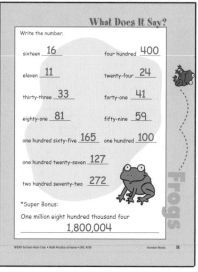

Page 12

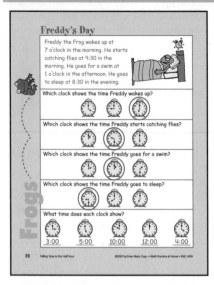

Page 13

Page 14

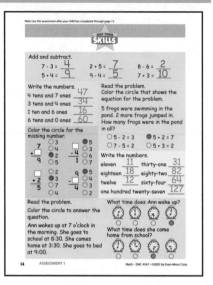

Page 15

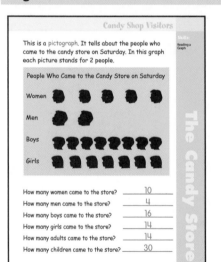

Page 16

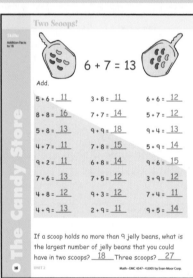

Page 17

Page 18

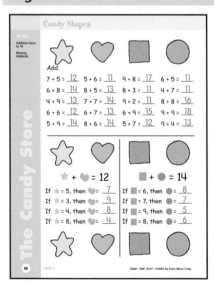

Page 19

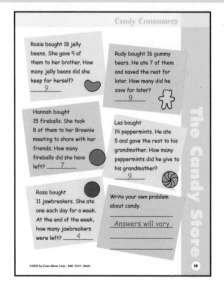

Page 20

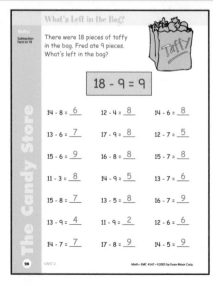

Page 21

Page 22

Page 23

Page 24

Page 25

Page 26

Page 27

Page 28

Page 29

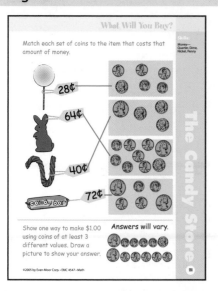

What Will You Buy?

Match each set of coins to the item that costs that amount of money.

28¢
64¢
40¢
72¢

Show one way to make $1.00 using coins of at least 3 different values. Draw a picture to show your answer.

Answers will vary.

©2005 by Evan-Moor Corp. • EMC 4547 • Math — 21

Lollipop, Lollipop

$3 + 2 + 2 = 7$

Add.

$2 + 1 + 3 = \underline{6}$ $1 + 4 + 3 = \underline{8}$ $7 + 2 + 0 = \underline{9}$

$4 + 0 + 5 = \underline{9}$ $5 + 0 + 5 = \underline{10}$ $5 + 1 + 4 = \underline{10}$

$6 + 1 + 2 = \underline{9}$ $2 + 2 + 2 = \underline{6}$ $2 + 5 + 2 = \underline{9}$

$5 + 2 + 3 = \underline{10}$ $1 + 5 + 1 = \underline{7}$ $4 + 3 + 1 = \underline{8}$

$3 + 3 + 3 = \underline{9}$ $3 + 1 + 1 = \underline{5}$ $8 + 1 + 1 = \underline{10}$

$2 + 6 + 2 = \underline{10}$ $7 + 2 + 1 = \underline{10}$ $1 + 3 + 3 = \underline{7}$

If 4 boys and 4 girls each had 1 lollipop in each hand, how many lollipops did they have in all? __16__

22 — UNIT 2 — Math • EMC 4547 • ©2005 by Evan-Moor Corp.

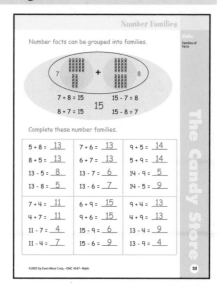

Number Families

Number facts can be grouped into families.

7 + 8
$7 + 8 = 15$ $15 - 7 = 8$
15
$8 + 7 = 15$ $15 - 8 = 7$

Complete these number families.

$5 + 8 = \underline{13}$	$7 + 6 = \underline{13}$	$9 + 5 = \underline{14}$
$8 + 5 = \underline{13}$	$6 + 7 = \underline{13}$	$5 + 9 = \underline{14}$
$13 - 5 = \underline{8}$	$13 - 7 = \underline{6}$	$14 - 9 = \underline{5}$
$13 - 8 = \underline{5}$	$13 - 6 = \underline{7}$	$14 - 5 = \underline{9}$
$7 + 4 = \underline{11}$	$6 + 9 = \underline{15}$	$9 + 4 = \underline{13}$
$4 + 7 = \underline{11}$	$9 + 6 = \underline{15}$	$4 + 9 = \underline{13}$
$11 - 7 = \underline{4}$	$15 - 9 = \underline{6}$	$13 - 4 = \underline{9}$
$11 - 4 = \underline{7}$	$15 - 6 = \underline{9}$	$13 - 9 = \underline{4}$

©2005 by Evan-Moor Corp. • EMC 4547 • Math — 23

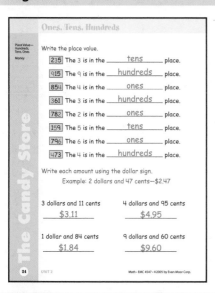

Ones, Tens, Hundreds

Write the place value.

235 The 3 is in the __tens__ place.
915 The 9 is in the __hundreds__ place.
854 The 4 is in the __ones__ place.
361 The 3 is in the __hundreds__ place.
782 The 2 is in the __ones__ place.
159 The 5 is in the __tens__ place.
796 The 6 is in the __ones__ place.
473 The 4 is in the __hundreds__ place.

Write each amount using the dollar sign.
Example: 2 dollars and 47 cents—$2.47

3 dollars and 11 cents
__$3.11__

4 dollars and 95 cents
__$4.95__

1 dollar and 84 cents
__$1.84__

9 dollars and 60 cents
__$9.60__

24 — UNIT 2 — Math • EMC 4547 • ©2005 by Evan-Moor Corp.

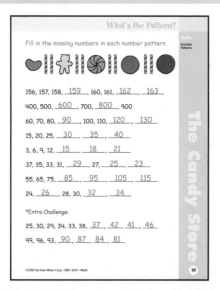

What's the Pattern?

Fill in the missing numbers in each number pattern.

156, 157, 158, __159__, 160, 161, __162__, __163__

400, 500, __600__, 700, __800__, 900

60, 70, 80, __90__, 100, 110, __120__, __130__

15, 20, 25, __30__, __35__, __40__

3, 6, 9, 12, __15__, __18__, __21__

37, 35, 33, 31, __29__, 27, __25__, __23__

55, 65, 75, __85__, __95__, __105__, __115__

24, __26__, 28, 30, __32__, __34__

*Extra Challenge:

25, 30, 29, 34, 33, 38, __37__, __42__, __41__, __46__

99, 96, 93, __90__, __87__, __84__, __81__

©2005 by Evan-Moor Corp. • EMC 4547 • Math — 25

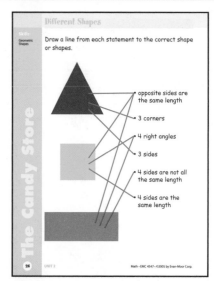

Different Shapes

Draw a line from each statement to the correct shape or shapes.

opposite sides are the same length
3 corners
4 right angles
3 sides
4 sides are not all the same length
4 sides are the same length

26 — UNIT 2 — Math • EMC 4547 • ©2005 by Evan-Moor Corp.

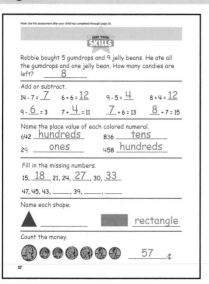

Note: Use this assessment after your child has completed through page 26.

TEST YOUR SKILLS

Robbie bought 5 gumdrops and 9 jelly beans. He ate all the gumdrops and one jelly bean. How many candies are left? __8__

Add or subtract.

$14 - 7 = \underline{7}$ $6 + 6 = \underline{12}$ $9 - 5 = \underline{4}$ $8 + 4 = \underline{12}$

$9 - \underline{6} = 3$ $7 + \underline{4} = 11$ $\underline{7} + 6 = 13$ $\underline{8} + 7 = 15$

Name the place value of each colored numeral.

642 __hundreds__   836 __tens__
29 __ones__   458 __hundreds__

Fill in the missing numbers.

15, __18__, 21, 24, __27__, 30, __33__

47, 45, 43, ____, 39, ___, ___

Name each shape.

▲ _____   ▬ __rectangle__

Count the money.

__57__ ¢

27

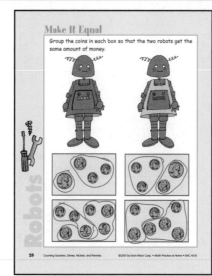

Make It Equal

Group the coins in each box so that the two robots get the same amount of money.

28 — Counting Quarters, Dimes, Nickels, and Pennies — ©2001 by Evan-Moor Corp. • Math Practice at Home • EMC 4518

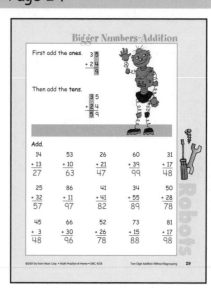

Bigger Numbers-Addition

First add the ones.
```
  3 5
+ 2 4
    9
```

Then add the tens.
```
  3 5
+ 2 4
  5 9
```

Add.

14	53	26	60	31
+ 13	+ 10	+ 21	+ 39	+ 17
27	63	47	99	48

25	86	41	34	50
+ 32	+ 11	+ 41	+ 55	+ 28
57	97	82	89	78

45	66	52	73	81
+ 3	+ 30	+ 26	+ 15	+ 17
48	96	78	88	98

©2001 by Evan-Moor Corp. • Math Practice at Home • EMC 4518 — Two-Digit Addition Without Regrouping — 29

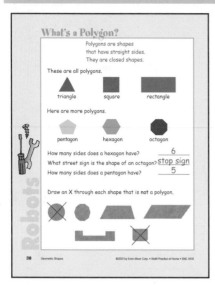

What's a Polygon?

Polygons are shapes that have straight sides. They are closed shapes.

These are all polygons.

triangle   square   rectangle

Here are more polygons.

pentagon   hexagon   octagon

How many sides does a hexagon have? __6__
What street sign is the shape of an octagon? __stop sign__
How many sides does a pentagon have? __5__

Draw an X through each shape that is not a polygon.

Bigger Numbers–Subtraction

First subtract the ones.
```
  2 8
- 1 5
    3
```

Then subtract the tens.
```
  2 8
- 1 5
  1 3
```

Subtract.

73	48	47	26	77
- 50	- 17	- 11	- 20	- 54
23	31	36	6	23

85	23	64	39	50
- 42	- 11	- 53	- 16	- 30
43	12	11	23	20

55	43	88	69	36
- 13	- 22	- 35	- 47	- 20
42	21	53	22	16

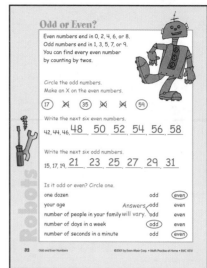

Odd or Even?

Even numbers end in 0, 2, 4, 6, or 8.
Odd numbers end in 1, 3, 5, 7, or 9.
You can find every even number by counting by twos.

Circle the odd numbers.
Make an X on the even numbers.

(17) ✗ (35) ✗ (59)

Write the next six even numbers.

42, 44, 46, __48__ __50__ __52__ __54__ __56__ __58__

Write the next six odd numbers.

15, 17, 19, __21__ __23__ __25__ __27__ __29__ __31__

Is it odd or even? Circle one.

one dozen		odd	(even)
your age	Answers	odd	even
number of people in your family	will vary.	odd	even
number of days in a week		(odd)	even
number of seconds in a minute		odd	(even)

Just Regroup–Adding

```
 56      1        1
+ 7     56       56
        + 7      + 7
          3       63
Add the    Write the 3    Add the
ones.      ones. Move     tens.
           the ten to
           the tens place.
```

Add.

24	36	43	57	48
+ 8	+ 5	+ 7	+ 4	+ 9
32	41	50	61	57

64	29	75	19	33
+ 7	+ 1	+ 7	+ 6	+ 9
71	30	82	25	42

43	52	38	65	76
+ 8	+ 9	+ 7	+ 5	+ 6
51	61	45	70	82

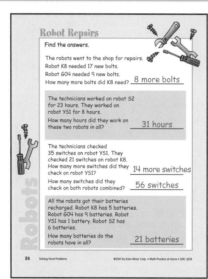

Robot Repairs

Find the answers.

The robots went to the shop for repairs.
Robot K8 needed 17 new bolts.
Robot G04 needed 9 new bolts.
How many more bolts did K8 need? __8 more bolts__

The technicians worked on robot S2 for 23 hours. They worked on robot YS1 for 8 hours.
How many hours did they work on these two robots in all? __31 hours__

The technicians checked 35 switches on robot YS1. They checked 21 switches on robot K8.
How many more switches did they check on robot YS1? __14 more switches__
How many switches did they check on both robots combined? __56 switches__

All the robots got their batteries recharged. Robot K8 has 5 batteries. Robot G04 has 9 batteries. Robot YS1 has 1 battery. Robot S2 has 6 batteries.
How many batteries do the robots have in all? __21 batteries__

Comparing Numbers

Write > or < between each pair of numbers.

means greater than
9 > 2

14	<	27
81	>	66
25	>	19
36	<	42
100	<	110
163	<	197
435	>	316
652	>	228
94	<	103

means less than
1 < 5

Use > or < to make each sentence true.

1. The number of keys on a piano is __>__ the number of strings on a guitar.
2. The number of days in February is __<__ the number of days in March.
3. The number of inches in a foot is __<__ the number of cards in a deck.

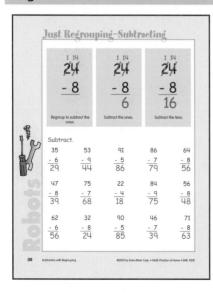

Just Regrouping–Subtracting

```
 1 14    1 14    1 14
  24      24      24
 - 8     - 8     - 8
           6      16
Regroup to   Subtract    Subtract
subtract     the ones.   the tens.
the ones.
```

Subtract.

35	53	91	86	64
- 6	- 9	- 5	- 7	- 8
29	44	86	79	56

47	75	22	84	56
- 8	- 7	- 4	- 9	- 8
39	68	18	75	48

62	32	90	46	71
- 6	- 8	- 5	- 7	- 8
56	24	85	39	63

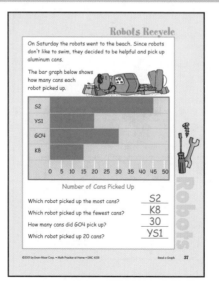

Robots Recycle

On Saturday the robots went to the beach. Since robots don't like to swim, they decided to be helpful and pick up aluminum cans.

The bar graph below shows how many cans each robot picked up.

S2										
YS1										
G04										
K8										

0   5   10   15   20   25   30   35   40   45   50

Number of Cans Picked Up

Which robot picked up the most cans? __S2__
Which robot picked up the fewest cans? __K8__
How many cans did G04 pick up? __30__
Which robot picked up 20 cans? __YS1__

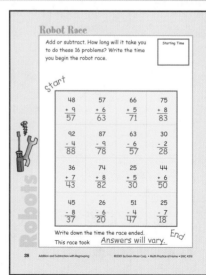

Robot Race

Add or subtract. How long will it take you to do these 16 problems? Write the time you begin the robot race.

Starting Time

Start

48	57	66	75
+ 9	+ 6	+ 5	+ 8
57	63	71	83

92	87	63	30
- 4	- 9	- 6	- 2
88	78	57	28

36	74	25	44
+ 7	+ 8	+ 5	+ 6
43	82	30	50

45	26	51	25
- 8	- 6	- 4	- 7
37	20	47	18

End

Write down the time the race ended.
This race took __Answers will vary.__

134

Math • EMC 4547 • © Evan-Moor Corp.

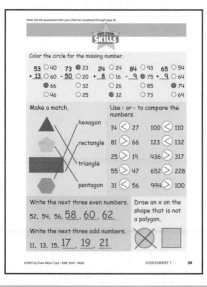

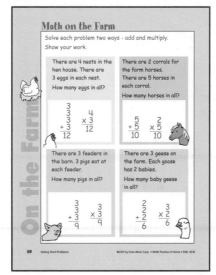

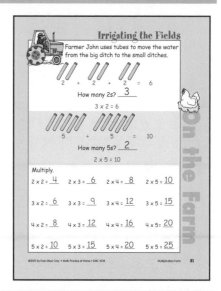

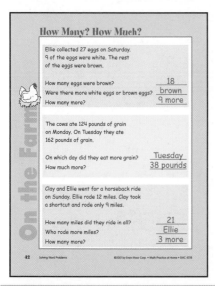

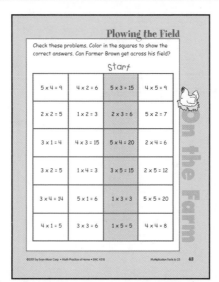

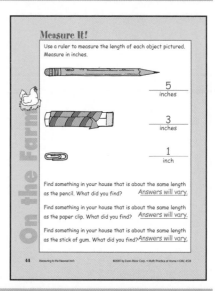

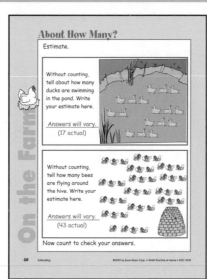

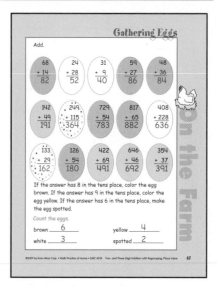

© Evan-Moor Corp. • EMC 4547 • Math

135

Page 48

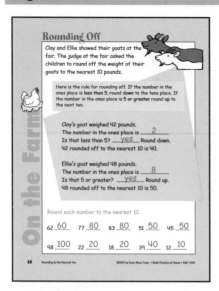

Rounding Off

Clay and Ellie showed their goats at the fair. The judge at the fair asked the children to round off the weight of their goats to the nearest 10 pounds.

Here is the rule for rounding off. If the number in the ones place is less than 5, round down to the tens place. If the number in the ones place is 5 or greater, round up to the next ten.

Clay's goat weighed 42 pounds.
The number in the ones place is __2__
Is that less than 5? __yes__ Round down.
42 rounded off to the nearest 10 is 40.

Ellie's goat weighed 48 pounds.
The number in the ones place is __8__
Is that 5 or greater? __yes__ Round up.
48 rounded off to the nearest 10 is 50.

Round each number to the nearest 10.

62 __60__   77 __80__   83 __80__   51 __50__   45 __50__

98 __100__   22 __20__   18 __20__   39 __40__   12 __10__

Page 49

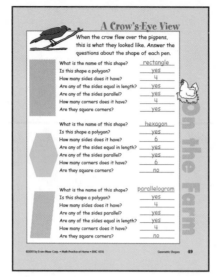

A Crow's-Eye View

When the crow flew over the pigpens, this is what they looked like. Answer the questions about the shape of each pen.

What is the name of this shape? __rectangle__
Is this shape a polygon? __yes__
How many sides does it have? __4__
Are any of the sides equal in length? __yes__
Are any of the sides parallel? __yes__
How many corners does it have? __4__
Are they square corners? __yes__

What is the name of this shape? __hexagon__
Is this shape a polygon? __yes__
How many sides does it have? __6__
Are any of the sides equal in length? __yes__
Are any of the sides parallel? __yes__
How many corners does it have? __6__
Are they square corners? __no__

What is the name of this shape? __parallelogram__
Is this shape a polygon? __yes__
How many sides does it have? __4__
Are any of the sides parallel? __yes__
Are any of the sides equal in length? __yes__
How many corners does it have? __4__
Are they square corners? __no__

Page 50

Counting the Bales

Farmer Jones records the number of hay bales in each of his stacks. He has the numbers for the first and second cuttings. Add the numbers together to see which stack has the most bales.

367	224	316	408	149
+ 128	+ 349	+ 57	+ 366	+ 239
495	573	373	774	388

157	(906)	245	567	626
+ 628	+ 77	+ 435	+ 239	+ 256
785	983	680	806	882

433	628	553	189	365
+ 248	+ 155	+ 409	+ 112	+ 617
681	783	962	301	982

Circle the stack that has the most bales.

Page 51

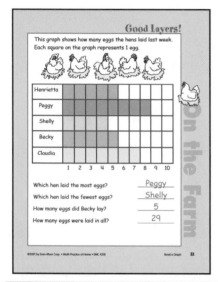

Good Layers!

This graph shows how many eggs the hens laid last week. Each square on the graph represents 1 egg.

Henrietta										
Peggy										
Shelly										
Becky										
Claudia										

Which hen laid the most eggs? __Peggy__
Which hen laid the fewest eggs? __Shelly__
How many eggs did Becky lay? __5__
How many eggs were laid in all? __29__

Page 52

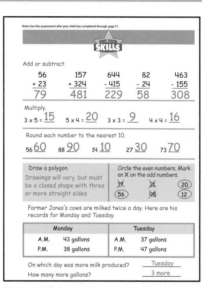

Note: Use this assessment after your child has completed through page 51.

TEST YOUR SKILLS

Add or subtract.

56	157	644	82	463
+ 23	+ 324	- 415	- 24	- 155
79	481	229	58	308

Multiply.

$3 \times 5 = $ __15__ $5 \times 4 = $ __20__ $3 \times 3 = $ __9__ $4 \times 4 = $ __16__

Round each number to the nearest 10.

56 __60__   88 __90__   14 __10__   27 __30__   73 __70__

Draw a polygon.
Drawings will vary, but must be a closed shape with three or more straight sides

Circle the even numbers. Mark an X on the odd numbers.
X 35   X 31   (20)
(56)   X 95   (12)

Farmer Jones's cows are milked twice a day. Here are his records for Monday and Tuesday.

Monday		Tuesday	
A.M.	43 gallons	A.M.	37 gallons
P.M.	38 gallons	P.M.	47 gallons

On which day was more milk produced? __Tuesday__
How many more gallons? __3 more__

Page 53

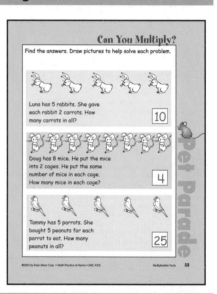

Can You Multiply?

Find the answers. Draw pictures to help solve each problem.

Luna has 5 rabbits. She gave each rabbit 2 carrots. How many carrots in all? **10**

Doug has 8 mice. He put the mice into 2 cages. He put the same number of mice in each cage. How many mice in each cage? **4**

Tammy has 5 parrots. She bought 5 peanuts for each parrot to eat. How many peanuts in all? **25**

Page 54

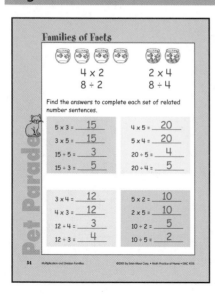

Families of Facts

4 × 2   2 × 4
8 ÷ 2   8 ÷ 4

Find the answers to complete each set of related number sentences.

$5 \times 3 = $ __15__ $4 \times 5 = $ __20__
$3 \times 5 = $ __15__ $5 \times 4 = $ __20__
$15 \div 5 = $ __3__ $20 \div 5 = $ __4__
$15 \div 3 = $ __5__ $20 \div 4 = $ __5__

$3 \times 4 = $ __12__ $5 \times 2 = $ __10__
$4 \times 3 = $ __12__ $2 \times 5 = $ __10__
$12 \div 4 = $ __3__ $10 \div 2 = $ __5__
$12 \div 3 = $ __4__ $10 \div 5 = $ __2__

Page 55

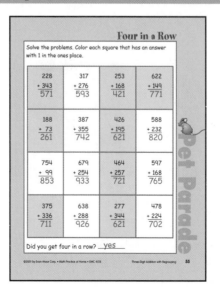

Four in a Row

Solve the problems. Color each square that has an answer with 1 in the ones place.

228	317	253	622
+ 343	+ 276	+ 168	+ 149
571	593	421	771

188	387	426	588
+ 73	+ 355	+ 195	+ 232
261	742	621	820

754	679	464	597
+ 99	+ 254	+ 257	+ 168
853	933	721	765

375	638	277	478
+ 336	+ 288	+ 344	+ 224
711	926	621	702

Did you get four in a row? __yes__

Page 56

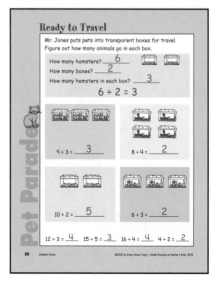

Ready to Travel

Mr. Jones puts pets into transparent boxes for travel. Figure out how many animals go in each box.

How many hamsters? __6__
How many boxes? __2__
How many hamsters in each box? __3__

$6 \div 2 = 3$

$9 \div 3 = $ __3__ $8 \div 4 = $ __2__

$10 \div 2 = $ __5__ $6 \div 3 = $ __2__

$12 \div 3 = $ __4__ $15 \div 5 = $ __3__ $16 \div 4 = $ __4__ $4 \div 2 = $ __2__

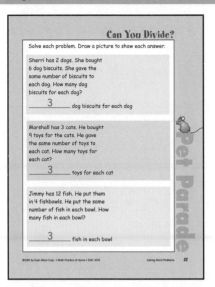

Page 57 — Can You Divide?

Solve each problem. Draw a picture to show each answer.

Sherri has 2 dogs. She bought 6 dog biscuits. She gave the same number of biscuits to each dog. How many dog biscuits for each dog?

___3___ dog biscuits for each dog

Marshall has 3 cats. He bought 9 toys for the cats. He gave the same number of toys to each cat. How many toys for each cat?

___3___ toys for each cat

Jimmy has 12 fish. He put them in 4 fishbowls. He put the same number of fish in each bowl. How many fish in each bowl?

___3___ fish in each bowl

Page 58 — Just Add It!

659	425	794	832
+ 156	+ 284	+ 67	+ 139
815	709	861	971

556	942	277	195
+ 375	+ 58	+ 646	+ 591
931	1000	923	786

318	263	678	373
+ 482	+ 470	+ 35	+ 239
800	733	713	612

289	555	499	367
+ 546	+ 387	+ 421	+ 103
835	942	920	470

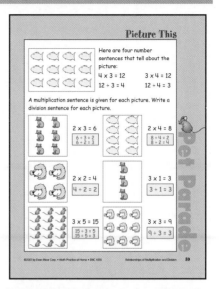

Page 59 — Picture This

Here are four number sentences that tell about the picture:

4 × 3 = 12   3 × 4 = 12
12 ÷ 3 = 4   12 ÷ 4 = 3

A multiplication sentence is given for each picture. Write a division sentence for each picture.

2 × 3 = 6   → 6 ÷ 3 = 2 / 6 ÷ 2 = 3
2 × 4 = 8   → 8 ÷ 4 = 2 / 8 ÷ 2 = 4
2 × 2 = 4   → 4 ÷ 2 = 2
3 × 1 = 3   → 3 ÷ 1 = 3
3 × 5 = 15 → 15 ÷ 3 = 5 / 15 ÷ 5 = 3
3 × 3 = 9   → 9 ÷ 3 = 3

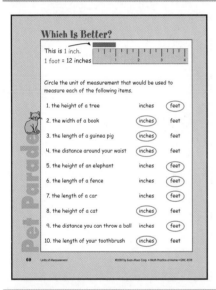

Page 60 — Which Is Better?

This is 1 inch.
1 foot = 12 inches

Circle the unit of measurement that would be used to measure each of the following items.

1. the height of a tree — inches (feet)
2. the width of a book — (inches) feet
3. the length of a guinea pig — (inches) feet
4. the distance around your waist — (inches) feet
5. the height of an elephant — inches (feet)
6. the length of a fence — inches (feet)
7. the length of a car — inches (feet)
8. the height of a cat — (inches) feet
9. the distance you can throw a ball — inches (feet)
10. the length of your toothbrush — (inches) feet

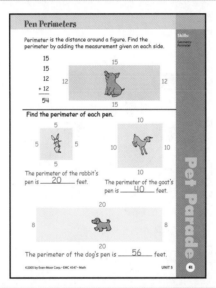

Page 61 — Pen Perimeters

Perimeter is the distance around a figure. Find the perimeter by adding the measurement given on each side.

```
  15
  15
+ 12
  ——
  54
```
(sides 12, 12, 15, 15)

Find the perimeter of each pen.

Rabbit pen: 5, 5, 5, 5
The perimeter of the rabbit's pen is ___20___ feet.

Goat pen: 10, 10, 10, 10
The perimeter of the goat's pen is ___40___ feet.

Dog pen: 8, 8, 20, 20
The perimeter of the dog's pen is ___56___ feet.

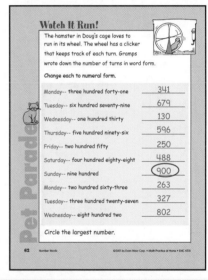

Page 62 — Watch It Run!

The hamster in Doug's cage loves to run in its wheel. The wheel has a clicker that keeps track of each turn. Gramps wrote down the number of turns in word form.

Change each to numeral form.

Monday-- three hundred forty-one	341
Tuesday-- six hundred seventy-nine	679
Wednesday-- one hundred thirty	130
Thursday-- five hundred ninety-six	596
Friday-- two hundred fifty	250
Saturday-- four hundred eighty-eight	488
Sunday-- nine hundred	(900)
Monday-- two hundred sixty-three	263
Tuesday-- three hundred twenty-seven	327
Wednesday-- eight hundred two	802

Circle the largest number.

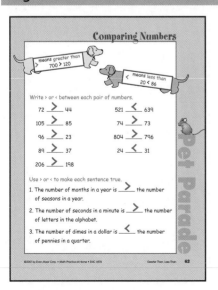

Page 63 — Comparing Numbers

> means greater than
700 > 120

< means less than
20 < 86

Write > or < between each pair of numbers.

72 > 44   521 < 639
105 > 85   74 > 73
96 > 23   804 > 796
89 > 37   24 < 31
206 > 198

Use > or < to make each sentence true.

1. The number of months in a year is < the number of seasons in a year.
2. The number of seconds in a minute is > the number of letters in the alphabet.
3. The number of dimes in a dollar is < the number of pennies in a quarter.

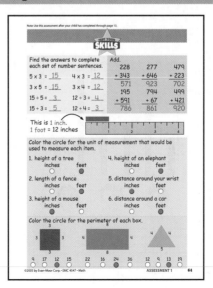

Page 64 — SKILLS

Note: Use this assessment after your child has completed through page 13.

Find the answers to complete each set of number sentences.

5 × 3 = 15   4 × 3 = 12
3 × 5 = 15   3 × 4 = 12
15 ÷ 5 = 3   12 ÷ 3 = 4
15 ÷ 3 = 5   12 ÷ 4 = 3

Add.

228	277	479
+ 343	+ 646	+ 223
571	923	702

195	794	499
+ 591	+ 67	+ 421
786	861	920

This is 1 inch.
1 foot = 12 inches

Color the circle for the unit of measurement that would be used to measure each item.

1. height of a tree — inches / feet
2. length of a fence — inches / feet
3. height of a mouse — inches / feet
4. height of an elephant — inches / feet
5. distance around your wrist — inches / feet
6. distance around a car — inches / feet

Color the circle for the perimeter of each box.

3 3 → 9 12 15
4 4 → 22 16 24
4 5 → 13 19

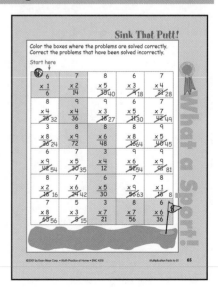

Page 65 — Sink That Putt!

Color the boxes where the problems are solved correctly. Correct the problems that have been solved incorrectly.

Start here

6 ×1 = 6	7 ×2 = 14	8 ×5 = 30/40	6 ×3 = 18	4 ×4 = 21/28
8 ×4 = 26/32	9 ×4 = 36	3 ×9 = 18/27	5 ×6 = 30	7 ×7 = 42/49
3 ×8 = 26/24	8 ×9 = 72	6 ×8 = 48	8 ×2 = 16/64	5 ×9 = 40/45
6 ×9 = 42/54	5 ×7 = 30/35	4 ×3 = 12	6 ×9 = 52/54	9 ×9 = 91/81
8 ×2 = 18/16	6 ×4 = 24/42	5 ×6 = 30	9 ×7 = 56/63	1 ×8 = 18/8
7 ×8 = 65/56	5 ×3 = 9/15	3 ×7 = 21	7 ×7 = 56	6 ×6 = 36

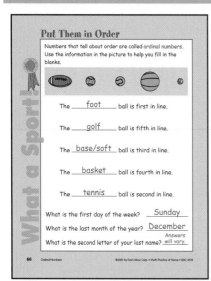

Put Them in Order

Numbers that tell about order are called ordinal numbers. Use the information in the picture to help you fill in the blanks.

The ___foot___ ball is first in line.

The ___golf___ ball is fifth in line.

The ___base/soft___ ball is third in line.

The ___basket___ ball is fourth in line.

The ___tennis___ ball is second in line.

What is the first day of the week? ___Sunday___

What is the last month of the year? ___December___

What is the second letter of your last name? ___will vary___ (Answers)

66 Ordinal Numbers ©2001 by Evan-Moor Corp. • Math Practice at Home • EMC 4518

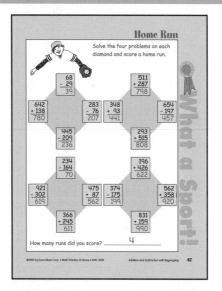

Home Run

Solve the four problems on each diamond and score a home run.

```
  68          511
- 29        + 287
  39          798

642   283   348    654
+138  - 76  + 93  - 197
 780   207   441    457

445          293
-209        +515
 236          808

234          196
-164        +426
  70          622

921   475   374    562
-302  + 87  -175  +358
 619   562   199    920

366          831
+245        +159
 611          990
```

How many runs did you score? ___4___

©2001 by Evan-Moor Corp. • Math Practice at Home • EMC 4518 Addition and Subtraction with Regrouping 67

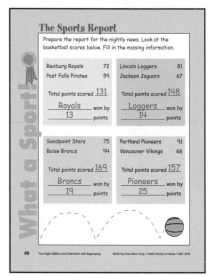

The Sports Report

Prepare the report for the nightly news. Look at the basketball scores below. Fill in the missing information.

| Rexburg Royals | 72 |
| Post Falls Pirates | 59 |

Total points scored ___131___

___Royals___ won by ___13___ points

| Lincoln Loggers | 81 |
| Jackson Jaguars | 67 |

Total points scored ___148___

___Loggers___ won by ___14___ points

| Sandpoint Stars | 75 |
| Boise Broncs | 94 |

Total points scored ___169___

___Broncs___ won by ___19___ points

| Portland Pioneers | 91 |
| Vancouver Vikings | 66 |

Total points scored ___157___

___Pioneers___ won by ___25___ points

68 Two-Digit Addition and Subtraction with Regrouping ©2001 by Evan-Moor Corp. • Math Practice at Home • EMC 4518

Use Your Head

Use estimation to decide if the answer makes sense.

18 80
16 27

There are 16 boys on William's swim team. There are 18 girls. How many swimmers in all?

Answer: about 80 swimmers

Does the answer make sense? ___no___

Jose scored 24 points in a basketball game on Friday. He scored 27 points in a basketball game on Saturday. How many points in all?

Answer: about 50 points

Does the answer make sense? ___yes___

Janine ran for 48 minutes on Monday. On Wednesday she ran for 39 minutes. On Friday she ran for 50 minutes. How many minutes in all?

Answer: about 100 minutes

Does the answer make sense? ___no___

Renee spent $4.75 on a ticket to a baseball game. She bought her friend a ticket, too. How much did she spend in all?

Answer: about $10.00

Does the answer make sense? ___yes___

Matt did 25 push-ups in the morning. He did 51 push-ups in the afternoon. How many push-ups in all?

Answer: about 75 push-ups

Does the answer make sense? ___yes___

©2001 by Evan-Moor Corp. • Math Practice at Home • EMC 4518 Estimation 69

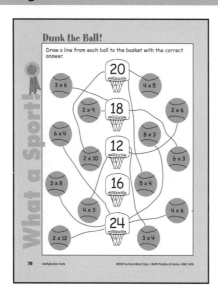

Dunk the Ball!

Draw a line from each ball to the basket with the correct answer.

20 — 3 × 6, 4 × 5
18 — 2 × 9, 2 × 6
12 — 6 × 4, 8 × 3
16 — 2 × 10, 6 × 3
24 — 3 × 8, 5 × 4, 4 × 3, 4 × 6, 2 × 12, 3 × 4

70 Multiplication Facts ©2001 by Evan-Moor Corp. • Math Practice at Home • EMC 4518

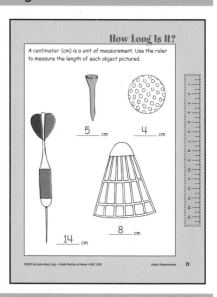

How Long Is It?

A centimeter (cm) is a unit of measurement. Use the ruler to measure the length of each object pictured.

___5___ cm   ___4___ cm

___14___ cm   ___8___ cm

©2001 by Evan-Moor Corp. • Math Practice at Home • EMC 4518 Metric Measurement 71

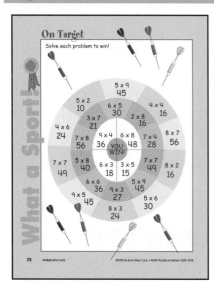

On Target

Solve each problem to win!

5 × 9 = 45
5 × 2 = 10
6 × 5 = 30
4 × 4 = 16
2 × 8 = 16
3 × 7 = 21
4 × 6 = 24
7 × 8 = 56
9 × 4 = 36
6 × 8 = 48
7 × 4 = 28
8 × 7 = 56
YOU WIN!
7 × 7 = 49
5 × 8 = 40
6 × 3 = 18
3 × 5 = 15
7 × 7 = 49
8 × 2 = 16
6 × 6 = 36
5 × 9 = 45
9 × 5 = 45
9 × 3 = 27
5 × 6 = 30
8 × 3 = 24

72 Multiplication Facts ©2001 by Evan-Moor Corp. • Math Practice at Home • EMC 4518

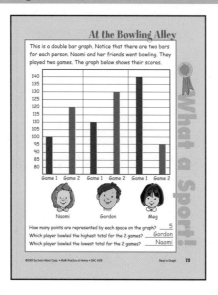

At the Bowling Alley

This is a double bar graph. Notice that there are two bars for each person. Naomi and her friends went bowling. They played two games. The graph below shows their scores.

Naomi Gordon Meg
Game 1 Game 2 Game 1 Game 2 Game 1 Game 2

How many points are represented by each space on the graph? ___5___

Which player bowled the highest total for the 2 games? ___Gordon___

Which player bowled the lowest total for the 2 games? ___Naomi___

©2001 by Evan-Moor Corp. • Math Practice at Home • EMC 4518 Read a Graph 73

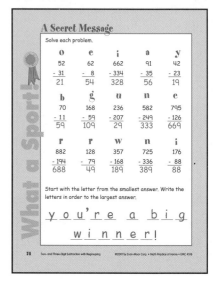

A Secret Message

Solve each problem.

```
  o      e      i      a      y
 52     62    662     91     42
-31    - 8   -334    -35    -23
 21     54    328     56     19

  b      g      u      n      e
 70    168    236    582    795
-11    -59   -207   -249   -126
 59    109     29    333    669

  r      r      w      n      i
882    128    357    725    176
-194   -79   -168   -336   - 88
688     49    189    389     88
```

Start with the letter from the smallest answer. Write the letters in order to the largest answer.

___y o u ' r e   a   b i g___

___w i n n e r !___

74 Two- and Three-Digit Subtraction with Regrouping ©2001 by Evan-Moor Corp. • Math Practice at Home • EMC 4518

138

Math • EMC 4547 • © Evan-Moor Corp.

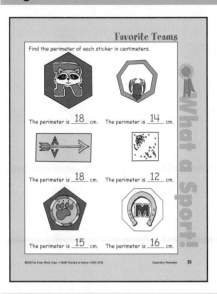

Favorite Teams

Find the perimeter of each sticker in centimeters.

The perimeter is **18** cm.
The perimeter is **14** cm.
The perimeter is **18** cm.
The perimeter is **12** cm.
The perimeter is **15** cm.
The perimeter is **16** cm.

©2001 by Evan-Moor Corp. • Math Practice at Home • EMC 4518   Geometry–Perimeter   75

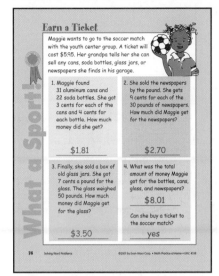

Earn a Ticket

Maggie wants to go to the soccer match with the youth center group. A ticket will cost $5.95. Her grandpa tells her she can sell any cans, soda bottles, glass jars, or newspapers she finds in his garage.

1. Maggie found 31 aluminum cans and 22 soda bottles. She got 3 cents for each of the cans and 4 cents for each bottle. How much money did she get?

$1.81

2. She sold the newspapers by the pound. She gets 9 cents for each of the 30 pounds of newspapers. How much did Maggie get for the newspapers?

$2.70

3. Finally, she sold a box of old glass jars. She got 7 cents a pound for the glass. The glass weighed 50 pounds. How much money did Maggie get for the glass?

$3.50

4. What was the total amount of money Maggie got for the bottles, cans, glass, and newspapers?

$8.01

Can she buy a ticket to the soccer match?

yes

76   Solving Word Problems   ©2001 by Evan-Moor Corp. • Math Practice at Home • EMC 4518

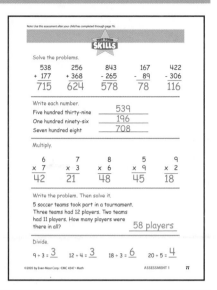

Note: Use this assessment after your child has completed through page 76.

TEST YOUR SKILLS

Solve the problems.

538	256	843	167	422
+ 177	+ 368	- 265	- 89	- 306
715	**624**	**578**	**78**	**116**

Write each number.
Five hundred thirty-nine   **539**
One hundred ninety-six   **196**
Seven hundred eight   **708**

Multiply.

6	7	8	5	9
× 7	× 3	× 6	× 9	× 2
42	**21**	**48**	**45**	**18**

Write the problem. Then solve it.

5 soccer teams took part in a tournament. Three teams had 12 players. Two teams had 11 players. How many players were there in all?   **58 players**

Divide.

$9 \div 3 = $ **3** $12 \div 4 = $ **3** $18 \div 3 = $ **6** $20 \div 5 = $ **4**

©2005 by Evan-Moor Corp. • EMC 4547 • Math   ASSESSMENT 1   77

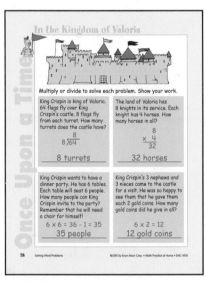

In the Kingdom of Valoria

Multiply or divide to solve each problem. Show your work.

King Crispin is king of Valoria. 64 flags fly over King Crispin's castle. 8 flags fly from each turret. How many turrets does the castle have?

8)‾64‾   **8 turrets**

The land of Valoria has 8 knights in its service. Each knight has 4 horses. How many horses in all?

8 × 4 = 32   **32 horses**

King Crispin wants to have a dinner party. He has 6 tables. Each table will seat 6 people. How many people can King Crispin invite to the party? Remember that he will need a chair for himself!

6 × 6 = 36 - 1 = 35   **35 people**

King Crispin's 3 nephews and 3 nieces came to the castle for a visit. He was so happy to see them that he gave them each 2 gold coins. How many gold coins did he give in all?

6 × 2 = 12   **12 gold coins**

78   Solving Word Problems   ©2001 by Evan-Moor Corp. • Math Practice at Home • EMC 4518

More About Valoria

King Crispin has 18 falcons. Each of his falconers trains 3 of the birds. How many falconers work for King Crispin?

3)‾18‾   **6 falconers**

King Crispin likes to play croquet. He plays for 2 hours every day, except for Sunday. How many hours does the king play croquet in a week?

6 × 2 = 12   **12 hours a week**

King Crispin loves to read books. Each week he adds 5 new books to his library. About how many books does he add each month?

5 × 4 = 20   **20 books**

The castle's art gallery is shaped like a square. There are 7 paintings on each wall. How many paintings in all?

7 × 4 = 28   **28 paintings**

©2001 by Evan-Moor Corp. • Math Practice at Home • EMC 4518   Solving Word Problems   79

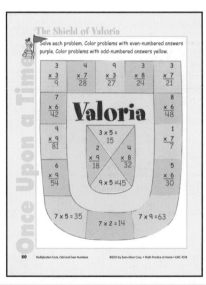

The Shield of Valoria

Solve each problem. Color problems with even-numbered answers purple. Color problems with odd-numbered answers yellow.

3	4	9	3	3
× 3	× 7	× 3	× 8	× 7
9	28	27	24	21

7				8
× 6				× 6
42				48

Valoria

3 × 5 = 15

9		4
× 9		× 8
81		32

| 1 |
| × 7 |
| 7 |

6		9 × 9 = 18		5
× 9				× 6
54				30

9 × 5 = 45

7 × 5 = 35   7 × 2 = 14   7 × 9 = 63

80   Multiplication Facts, Odd and Even Numbers   ©2001 by Evan-Moor Corp. • Math Practice at Home • EMC 4518

How Warm Is It?

A thermometer is used to measure temperature. Some thermometers use the Fahrenheit scale. On most thermometers, each space counts for 2 degrees. This thermometer shows 72 degrees Fahrenheit.

72°F

On the Fahrenheit scale, water freezes at 32°. Water boils at 212°.

What temperature does each thermometer show? Circle to tell whether each temperature shown is cold or warm.

94°F cold (warm)
30°F (cold) warm
16°F (cold) warm
88°F cold (warm)

©2001 by Evan-Moor Corp. • Math Practice at Home • EMC 4518   Measurement–Temperature   81

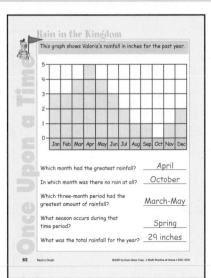

Rain in the Kingdom

This graph shows Valoria's rainfall in inches for the past year.

Which month had the greatest rainfall?   **April**
In which month was there no rain at all?   **October**
Which three-month period had the greatest amount of rainfall?   **March-May**
What season occurs during that time period?   **Spring**
What was the total rainfall for the year?   **29 inches**

82   Read a Graph   ©2001 by Evan-Moor Corp. • Math Practice at Home • EMC 4518

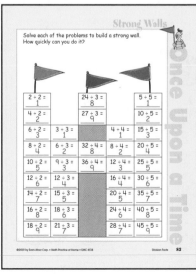

Strong Walls

Solve each of the problems to build a strong wall. How quickly can you do it?

$2 \div 2$ = 1	$24 \div 8$ = 3	$5 \div 5$ = 1
$4 \div 2$ = 2	$27 \div 3$ = 9	$10 \div 5$ = 2
$6 \div 2$ = 3	$3 \div 3$ = 1	$4 \div 4$ = 1	$15 \div 5$ = 3
$8 \div 2$ = 4	$6 \div 3$ = 2	$32 \div 4$ = 8	$8 \div 4$ = 2	$20 \div 5$ = 4
$10 \div 2$ = 5	$9 \div 3$ = 3	$36 \div 4$ = 9	$12 \div 4$ = 3	$25 \div 5$ = 5
$12 \div 2$ = 6	$12 \div 3$ = 4	$16 \div 4$ = 4	$30 \div 5$ = 6
$14 \div 2$ = 7	$15 \div 3$ = 5	$20 \div 4$ = 5	$35 \div 5$ = 7
$16 \div 2$ = 8	$18 \div 3$ = 6	$24 \div 4$ = 6	$40 \div 5$ = 8
$18 \div 2$ = 9	$21 \div 3$ = 7	$28 \div 4$ = 7	$45 \div 5$ = 9

©2001 by Evan-Moor Corp. • Math Practice at Home • EMC 4518   Division Facts   83

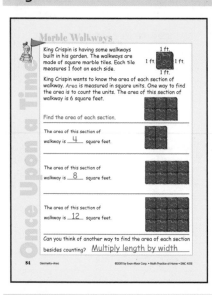

Marble Walkways

King Crispin is having some walkways built in his garden. The walkways are made of square marble tiles. Each tile measures 1 foot on each side.

1 ft.
1 ft. [tile] 1 ft.
1 ft.

King Crispin wants to know the area of each section of walkway. Area is measured in square units. One way to find the area is to count the units. The area of this section of walkway is 6 square feet.

Find the area of each section.

The area of this section of walkway is __4__ square feet.

The area of this section of walkway is __8__ square feet.

The area of this section of walkway is __12__ square feet.

Can you think of another way to find the area of each section besides counting? __Multiply length by width__

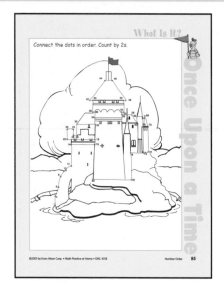

What Is It?

Connect the dots in order. Count by 2s.

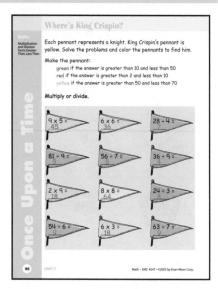

Where's King Crispin?

Each pennant represents a knight. King Crispin's pennant is yellow. Solve the problems and color the pennants to find him.

Make the pennant:
green if the answer is greater than 10 and less than 50
red if the answer is greater than 2 and less than 10
yellow if the answer is greater than 50 and less than 70

Multiply or divide.

9 × 5 = 45   6 × 6 = 36   28 ÷ 4 = 7
81 ÷ 9 = 9   56 ÷ 7 = 8   36 ÷ 9 = 4
2 × 9 = 18   8 × 8 = 64   24 ÷ 3 = 8
54 ÷ 6 = 9   6 × 3 = 18   63 ÷ 7 = 9

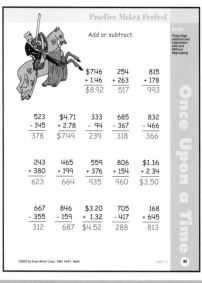

Practice Makes Perfect

Add or subtract.

$7.46 + 1.46 = $8.92	254 + 263 = 517	815 + 178 = 993
523 − 145 = 378	$4.71 + 2.78 = $7.49	333 − 94 = 239
685 − 367 = 318	832 − 466 = 366	
243 + 380 = 623	465 + 199 = 664	559 + 376 = 935
806 + 154 = 960	$1.16 + 2.34 = $3.50	
667 − 355 = 312	846 − 159 = 687	$3.20 + 1.32 = $4.52
705 − 417 = 288	168 + 645 = 813	

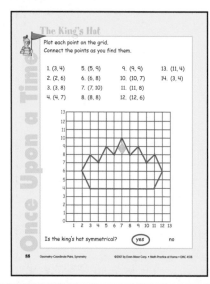

The King's Hat

Plot each point on the grid.
Connect the points as you find them.

1. (3, 4)   5. (5, 9)   9. (9, 9)   13. (11, 4)
2. (2, 6)   6. (6, 8)   10. (10, 7) 14. (3, 4)
3. (3, 8)   7. (7, 10) 11. (11, 8)
4. (4, 7)   8. (8, 8)   12. (12, 6)

Is the king's hat symmetrical?   (yes)   no

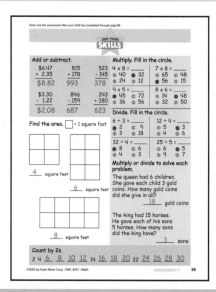

TEST YOUR SKILLS

Note: Use this assessment after your child has completed through page 88.

Add or subtract.
$6.47 + 2.35 = $8.82   815 + 178 = 993   523 − 145 = 378
$3.30 − 1.22 = $2.08   846 − 159 = 687   243 + 380 = 623

Multiply. Fill in the circle.
4 × 8 = ● 40 ○ 32   7 × 8 = ○ 65 ● 48
○ 24 ● 56   ● 56 ○ 15
9 × 5 = ● 45 ○ 72   8 × 6 = ○ 14 ● 48
○ 36 ● 56   ○ 32 ● 50

Divide. Fill in the circle.
6 ÷ 3 = ● 2 ○ 9   12 ÷ 4 = ○ 5 ● 3
○ 3 ● 18   ○ 4 ● 6
32 ÷ 4 = ● 8 ○ 6   25 ÷ 5 = ○ 6 ● 5
○ 4 ● 3   ● 9 ○ 7

Find the area. ☐ = 1 square foot
__4__ square feet
__6__ square feet
__8__ square feet

Multiply or divide to solve each problem.

The queen had 6 children. She gave each child 3 gold coins. How many gold coins did she give in all? __18__ gold coins

The king had 15 horses. He gave each of his sons 5 horses. How many sons did the king have? __3__ sons

Count by 2s.
2 4 __6__ __8__ 10 12 14 __16__ __18__ 20 22 __24__ __26__ __28__ __30__

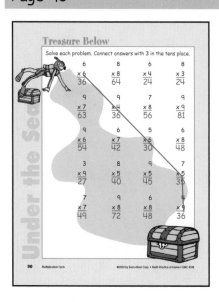

Treasure Below

Solve each problem. Connect answers with 3 in the tens place.

6 × 6 = 36   8 × 8 = 64   6 × 4 = 24   8 × 3 = 24
9 × 7 = 63   4 × 9 = 36   9 × 8 = 56   9 × 9 = 81
6 × 9 = 54   6 × 7 = 42   6 × 5 = 30   6 × 8 = 48
3 × 9 = 27   8 × 5 = 40   9 × 5 = 45   7 × 5 = 35
7 × 7 = 49   9 × 8 = 72   8 × 6 = 48   9 × 4 = 36

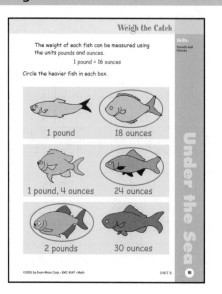

Weigh the Catch

The weight of each fish can be measured using the units pounds and ounces.

1 pound = 16 ounces

Circle the heavier fish in each box.

1 pound   18 ounces
1 pound, 4 ounces   24 ounces
2 pounds   30 ounces

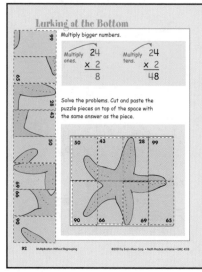

Lurking at the Bottom

Multiply bigger numbers.

Multiply 24 ones × 2 = 8   Multiply 24 tens × 2 = 48

Solve the problems. Cut and paste the puzzle pieces on top of the space with the same answer as the piece.

Math • EMC 4547 • © Evan-Moor Corp.

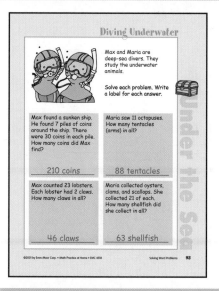

Diving Underwater

Max and Maria are deep-sea divers. They study the underwater animals.

Solve each problem. Write a label for each answer.

Max found a sunken ship. He found 7 piles of coins around the ship. There were 30 coins in each pile. How many coins did Max find?

210 coins

Maria saw 11 octopuses. How many tentacles (arms) in all?

88 tentacles

Max counted 23 lobsters. Each lobster had 2 claws. How many claws in all?

46 claws

Maria collected oysters, clams, and scallops. She collected 21 of each. How many shellfish did she collect in all?

63 shellfish

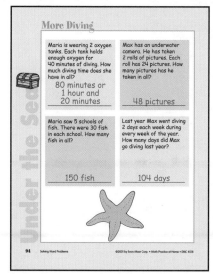

More Diving

Maria is wearing 2 oxygen tanks. Each tank holds enough oxygen for 40 minutes of diving. How much diving time does she have in all?

80 minutes or 1 hour and 20 minutes

Max has an underwater camera. He has taken 2 rolls of pictures. Each roll has 24 pictures. How many pictures has he taken in all?

48 pictures

Maria saw 5 schools of fish. There were 30 fish in each school. How many fish in all?

150 fish

Last year Max went diving 2 days each week during every week of the year. How many days did Max go diving last year?

104 days

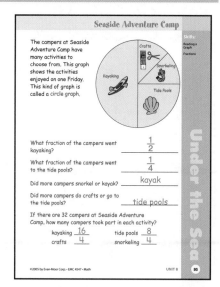

Seaside Adventure Camp

The campers at Seaside Adventure Camp have many activities to choose from. This graph shows the activities enjoyed on one Friday. This kind of graph is called a circle graph.

What fraction of the campers went kayaking?   **$\frac{1}{2}$**

What fraction of the campers went to the tide pools?   **$\frac{1}{4}$**

Did more campers snorkel or kayak?   **kayak**

Did more campers do crafts or go to the tide pools?   **tide pools**

If there are 32 campers at Seaside Adventure Camp, how many campers took part in each activity?

kayaking **16**   tide pools **8**
crafts **4**   snorkeling **4**

Divide It Evenly

Circle each number that can be divided evenly by 8.

(16) 15 (32)
(40) 52 (56)

8

Circle each number that can be divided evenly by 5.

(5) (10) 23
(35) (45) 39

5

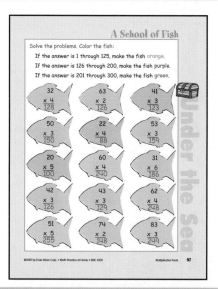

A School of Fish

Solve the problems. Color the fish:
If the answer is 1 through 125, make the fish orange.
If the answer is 126 through 200, make the fish purple.
If the answer is 201 through 300, make the fish green.

32 × 4 = **128**
63 × 2 = **126**
41 × 3 = **123**

50 × 3 = **150**
22 × 4 = **88**
53 × 3 = **159**

20 × 5 = **100**
60 × 4 = **240**
31 × 6 = **186**

42 × 3 = **126**
43 × 3 = **129**
62 × 4 = **248**

51 × 5 = **255**
74 × 2 = **148**
83 × 3 = **249**

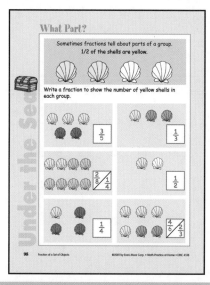

What Part?

Sometimes fractions tell about parts of a group.
1/2 of the shells are yellow.

Write a fraction to show the number of yellow shells in each group.

$\frac{3}{5}$

$\frac{1}{3}$

$\frac{2}{8}$ = $\frac{1}{4}$

$\frac{1}{2}$

$\frac{1}{4}$

$\frac{4}{6}$ = $\frac{2}{3}$

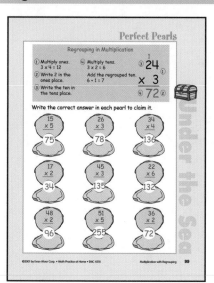

Perfect Pearls

Regrouping in Multiplication

① Multiply ones. 3 × 4 = 12
② Write 2 in the ones place.
③ Write the ten in the tens place.
④ Multiply tens. 3 × 2 = 6 Add the regrouped ten. 6 + 1 = 7

③ 2⁴ × 3 ④ 72 ②

Write the correct answer in each pearl to claim it.

15 × 5 = **75**
26 × 3 = **78**
34 × 4 = **136**

17 × 2 = **34**
45 × 3 = **135**
22 × 6 = **132**

48 × 2 = **96**
51 × 5 = **255**
36 × 2 = **72**

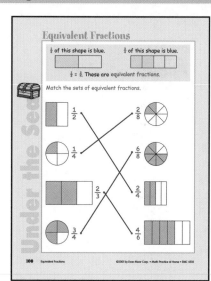

Equivalent Fractions

½ of this shape is blue.   ⅝ of this shape is blue.

½ = ⅝ These are equivalent fractions.

Match the sets of equivalent fractions.

$\frac{1}{2}$ $\frac{2}{8}$

$\frac{1}{4}$ $\frac{6}{8}$

$\frac{2}{3}$ $\frac{2}{4}$

$\frac{3}{4}$ $\frac{4}{6}$

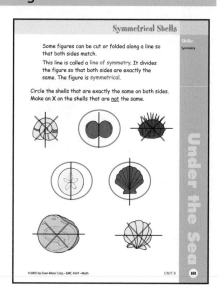

Symmetrical Shells

Some figures can be cut or folded along a line so that both sides match.

This line is called a line of symmetry. It divides the figure so that both sides are exactly the same. The figure is symmetrical.

Circle the shells that are exactly the same on both sides. Make an X on the shells that are <u>not</u> the same.

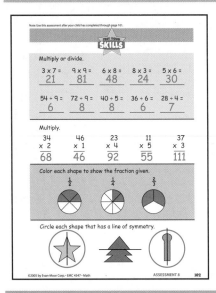

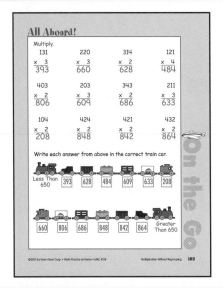

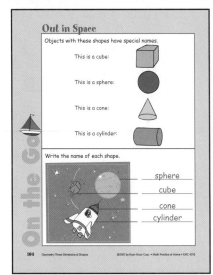

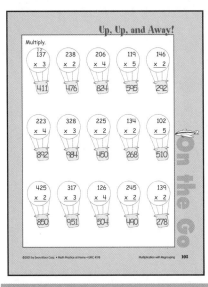

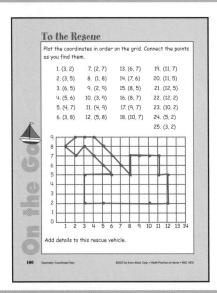

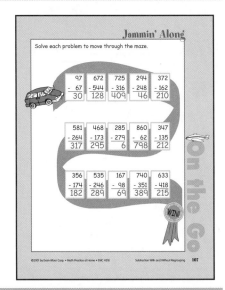

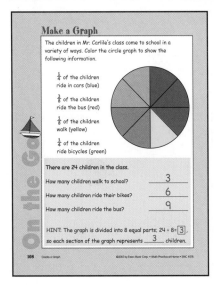

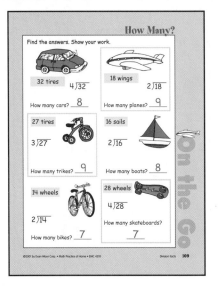

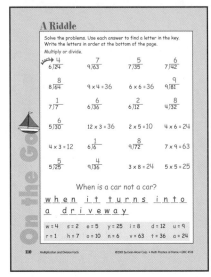

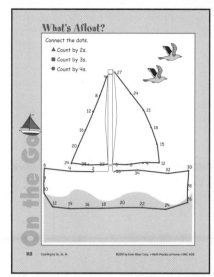

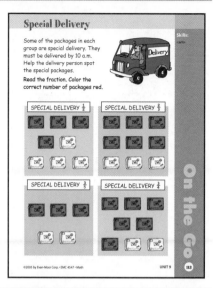

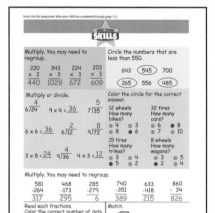

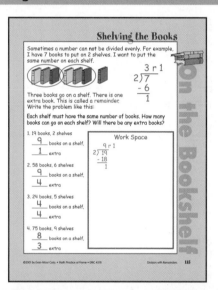

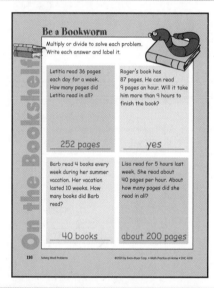

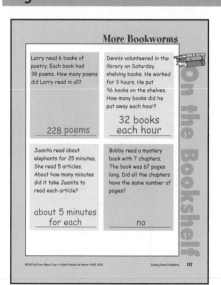

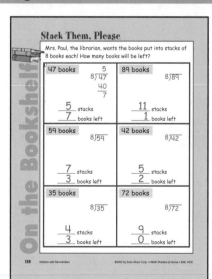

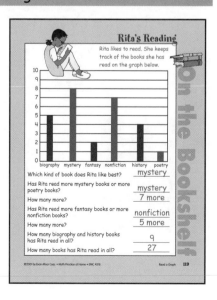

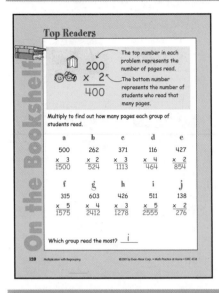

Top Readers

The top number in each problem represents the number of pages read.

$$\begin{array}{r} 200 \\ \times\ 2 \\ \hline 400 \end{array}$$

The bottom number represents the number of students who read that many pages.

Multiply to find out how many pages each group of students read.

a	b	c	d	e
500	262	371	116	427
× 3	× 2	× 3	× 4	× 2
1500	524	1113	464	854

f	g	h	i	j
315	603	426	511	138
× 5	× 4	× 3	× 5	× 2
1575	2412	1278	2555	276

Which group read the most? __i__

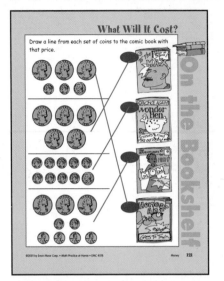

What Will It Cost?

Draw a line from each set of coins to the comic book with that price.

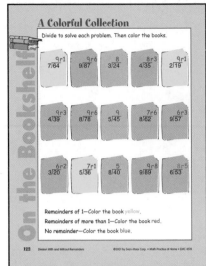

A Colorful Collection

Divide to solve each problem. Then color the books.

9r1 7)64	9r6 9)87	8 3)24	8r3 4)35	9r1 2)19
9r3 4)39	9r6 8)78	9 5)45	7r6 8)62	6r3 9)57
6r2 3)20	7r1 5)36	5 8)40	9r8 9)89	8r5 6)53

Remainders of 1—Color the book yellow.
Remainders of more than 1—Color the book red.
No remainder—Color the book blue.

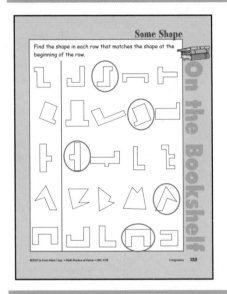

Same Shape

Find the shape in each row that matches the shape at the beginning of the row.

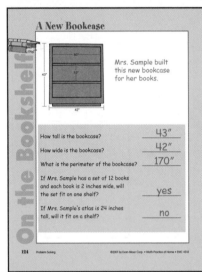

A New Bookcase

Mrs. Sample built this new bookcase for her books.

How tall is the bookcase?	43"
How wide is the bookcase?	42"
What is the perimeter of the bookcase?	170"
If Mrs. Sample has a set of 12 books and each book is 2 inches wide, will the set fit on one shelf?	yes
If Mrs. Sample's atlas is 24 inches tall, will it fit on a shelf?	no

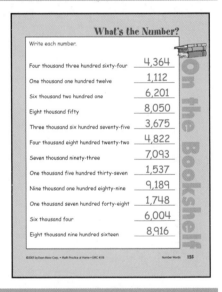

What's the Number?

Write each number.

Four thousand three hundred sixty-four	4,364
One thousand one hundred twelve	1,112
Six thousand two hundred one	6,201
Eight thousand fifty	8,050
Three thousand six hundred seventy-five	3,675
Four thousand eight hundred twenty-two	4,822
Seven thousand ninety-three	7,093
One thousand five hundred thirty-seven	1,537
Nine thousand one hundred eighty-nine	9,189
One thousand seven hundred forty-eight	1,748
Six thousand four	6,004
Eight thousand nine hundred sixteen	8,916

Fractions

Each shelf holds 10 books. Some of the books are checked out. Write a fraction that tells what part of each shelf's books are checked out.

$\frac{6}{10}$ or $\frac{3}{5}$

$\frac{2}{10}$ or $\frac{1}{5}$

$\frac{9}{10}$

$\frac{3}{10}$

$\frac{5}{10}$ or $\frac{1}{2}$

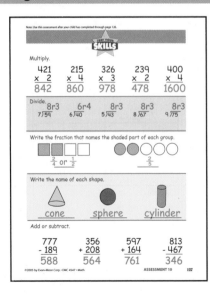

TEST YOUR SKILLS

Multiply.

421	215	326	239	400
× 2	× 4	× 3	× 2	× 4
842	860	978	478	1600

Divide.

8r3 7)59	6r4 6)40	8r3 5)43	8r3 8)67	8r3 9)75

Write the fraction that names the shaded part of each group.

$\frac{2}{4}$ or $\frac{1}{2}$ $\frac{2}{5}$

Write the name of each shape.

cone   sphere   cylinder

Add or subtract.

777	356	597	813
- 189	+ 208	+ 164	- 467
588	564	761	346

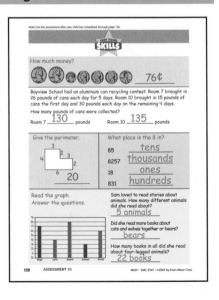

TEST YOUR SKILLS

How much money?   76¢

Bayview School had an aluminum can recycling contest. Room 7 brought in 26 pounds of cans each day for 5 days. Room 10 brought in 15 pounds of cans the first day and 30 pounds each day on the remaining 4 days. How many pounds of cans were collected?

Room 7 __130__ pounds   Room 10 __135__ pounds

Give the perimeter.   20

What place is the 8 in?

85	tens
8257	thousands
18	ones
831	hundreds

Read the graph. Answer the questions.

Sam loved to read stories about animals. How many different animals did she read about?
__5 animals__

Did she read more books about cats and wolves together or bears?
__bears__

How many books in all did she read about four-legged animals?
__22 books__